North Carolina By Rail

A Refreshingly Green Way to Travel
for Recreation, Business and Education

Information at your fingertips to plan and make trips on passenger trains in North Carolina

DAVID ROBINSON

ByRail Publishers
Raleigh

ByRail Publishers
P. O. Box 19417
Raleigh, NC 27619

www.byrail.info
byrail@gmx.com

ISBN 978-1-105-56710-2
1st Printing

Acknowledgement
This book is dedicated to my wife of 40 years, Ardyce, who has encouraged me to undertake many ventures that I would probably have never attempted on my own. Being a true daughter of her perfectionist father Frank Fischer (a Leo), she did not hesitate to express her opinions of the manuscript throughout its preparation, and contributed many ideas and corrections which I gladly incorporated. I also want to thank Tom Cook for his critical review of the final draft and thoughtful suggestions for improvement, as well as the entire staff (past and present) of the NCDOT's Rail Division who have so capably brought passenger train service to its current level of excellence and are, as you read this, implementing plans and projects to provide even better service in the near future. "May the Train Be With You!"

Contents

		Page
	Preface	5
Part 1	**Arriving in North Carolina**	7
	By Air	7
	By Train	8
	By Bus	9
	By Road	10
Part 2	**Taking the Train**	11
	One-Day Trips	14
	Trips with an Overnight Stay	18
	Special Event Stops	22
	Train & Bus Trips	22
	The Cost of Tickets	23
	Renting a Bicycle	24
Part 3	**What to See and Do**	27
	Burlington	27
	Cary	28
	Charlotte	31
	Durham	32
	Fayetteville	33
	Gastonia	35
	Greensboro	36
	Hamlet	37
	High Point	38
	Kannapolis	39
	Raleigh	40
	Rocky Mount	42
	Salisbury	44
	Selma	45
	Southern Pines	46
	Wilson	47
	Winston-Salem	49
Part 4	**Theme Trips**	51
Appendix A	Travel and Tourism Website Links	67
Appendix B	Banks and ATM's	69
Appendix C	Car Rental Locations	71
Appendix D	Colleges and Universities	73
Appendix E	Transportation Operators	77
Appendix F	Charlotte's Light Rail System, LYNX Blue Line	79
Appendix G	Checking Train Arrivals & Departures	81
	Index	83

CARY AMTRAK STATION, author photo

PASSENGERS BOARDING AT SELMA, author photo

Preface

"Sometimes You Need OPTIONS!" proclaims the State of North Carolina on its rail website (www.byrail.org), adding the fact that there are now "6 trains daily to Raleigh, Greensboro, Charlotte and 6 other NC Cities."

And options you certainly do have, ones that would not be available without the foresight and determination of the Rail Division of the North Carolina Department of Transportation (NCDOT) in cooperation with the National Railroad Passenger Corporation (Amtrak), the North Carolina Railroad Company (NCRR), and the two host freight railroads Norfolk Southern (NS) and CSX Transportation (CSXT).

The result is that a significant portion of the state and its communities and tourist attractions can now be conveniently reached by passenger trains.

It's pleasurable to have options, but passenger train travel in North Carolina generally still remains a mystery to many potential users, young and old, accustomed as they are to the convenience of their private vehicles. Where does the train go, where is the train station, what time does it depart, how long is the journey, how much does it cost, are the seats comfortable, how can I find my way around? All are valid questions that need answering before any decision is made to ride a train.

As known by citizens of other countries, the ability to travel from one city to another by train is not just characterized by the duration of the trip, but by the ability to perform many tasks (e.g., read a book, play a game, watch a movie, work, meet new people, take a walk to stretch your legs, snooze, etc.) that are either impossible or inadvisable to do when driving a vehicle and paying attention to all the other vehicles on the highway.

Train travel is for persons of all age groups. Taking a train trip may bring back fond memories for senior citizens and can make for an exciting day for a grandchild, but it is also a safer and more comfortable way to visit friends or family members in other cities. Youngsters below driving age, their parents, college students, business men and women and retirees can all find appealing aspects of train travel, if they just look into the option and give it a try.

The purpose of this book is to open your eyes to train travel in North Carolina, to reveal the opportunities it can give you, and to provide you with critical information that should make your trip planning fun and your travel pleasurable and rewarding.

GREENSBORO AMTRAK STATION (former Southern Railway Depot), author photo

FAYETTEVILLE AMTRAK STATION, author photo

Part 1

ARRIVING IN NORTH CAROLINA

This chapter is primarily for readers who do not already live in North Carolina, but even if you do there probably will be an interesting fact or two that you can take away. So read on to learn more.

Regardless of where you live in the USA, Canada or overseas, you'll be traveling to North Carolina by air, train, bus or road. Let's take a look at where you're likely to arrive by each of these modes of travel and how you get to a train station to start your travels by rail.

BY AIR

There are three major airports in North Carolina: **Raleigh-Durham** International (RDU) midway between Raleigh and Durham; **Piedmont Triad** International Airport (GSO) midway between Greensboro and Winston-Salem; and **Charlotte Douglas** International Airport (CLT) on the west side of Charlotte. Assuming you are not intending to rent a car (after all, this book is mostly about trains and public transportation), these three airports are served by taxicabs and local buses that can take you to the train station. However, if you think you will need to rent a car at some point during your trip, you can find information in Appendix C.

Raleigh-Durham International Airport (RDU) (www.rdu.com)

Triangle Transit (www.triangletransit.org) runs buses that will connect you with the **Amtrak** Station in Raleigh and the one in Durham. Route 100 (Raleigh- Airport-RTC) picks up at both Terminals 1 and 2 every 30 to 60 minutes depending on the time of day between 6:30am and 10:30pm. The bus going to Raleigh will deposit you at Moore Square (Bus) Station in Downtown Raleigh within 45 minutes. The Raleigh Amtrak Station is about an 8-block walk SW of Moore Square; it is also served by Capital Area Transit (CAT) Route 11 Avent Ferry, but you must state the Amtrak Station as your destination when you board the bus at Moore Square since it involves a minor route detour. The adult fare on CAT (www.raleighnc.gov/transit) is $1.00.

Catching a Triangle Transit bus going in the correct direction is important because the Route 100 bus from Raleigh also picks up at Terminals 1 and 2 on its way to the Regional Transportation Center (RTC) which is where you must go if your destination is Durham. To get to Durham you need to first ride Route 100 to the Regional Transportation Center where you then transfer to Route 700 (Durham-RTC). Ask the driver of the Route 100 bus for a (free) transfer ticket. The ride from the Airport to the RTC is 15 minutes and from the RTC to Durham (Bus) Station is about 40 minutes. The adult fare is $2.00. The Durham Amtrak Station is located across the railroad tracks from the Durham Bus Station, connected by a street underpass.

*HINT: The **GoTriangle** website (www.gotriangle.org) consolidates all of the bus service information for Raleigh, Cary, Durham and Chapel Hill and can be very helpful if you plan on traveling by bus within the Triangle Area.*

Piedmont Triad International Airport (GSO) (www.flyfrompti.com)

The Piedmont Authority for Regional Transportation (www.partnc.org) serves Piedmont Triad International Airport with its Express Shuttle No. 4. This bus will take you to the PART Hub where you will be able to transfer onto Express Route 3 (High Point) that can take you to the High Point Transit Center (adjacent to the High Point Amtrak Station) or Express Route 2 (Greensboro) that can take you to the Greensboro Transit Authority Center (next to the Greensboro Amtrak Station.) The adult fare for Routes 3 and 4 is $2.40; the Express Shuttle No. 4 is free. The trips to High Point and to Greensboro are each about 30 minutes and buses run between 6:00am and 6:30pm.

Charlotte Douglas International Airport (CLT) (www.charlotteairport.com)

The Charlotte Area Transit System (CATS) (www.ridetransit.org) runs Airport-Route 5 (also called "Sprinter") buses between the airport (Baggage Claim Zone D) and the Charlotte Transportation Center in Uptown Charlotte (a 25-minute ride) from 6am to midnight on weekdays and to 1am on the weekend. Route 5 departure frequencies vary from 20 minutes to 60 minutes depending on the time of day. The adult fare is $1.75 (exact change) – be sure to ask for a (free) transfer ticket.

To get to the Amtrak Station, which is 1 ½ miles NE of Uptown, you will need to transfer to the Route 11-North Tryon bus for a 6-minute ride. Route 11 departure frequencies vary from 10 minutes to 30 minutes depending on the time of day. Give your transfer ticket to the driver. Get off the bus at "Tryon & Dalton" – the Amtrak Station will be ahead of you on your right.

HINT: Since there is no food service at the Charlotte Amtrak Station, and if you have time, eat or pick up food in Uptown Charlotte (there are several close-by places) before boarding the Route 11 bus to the Amtrak Station; just don't eat or drink on the bus.

ARRIVING BY TRAIN

Amtrak provides daily passenger train service to North Carolina from three directions: (1) the northeast (including New York and Washington, DC), (2) Florida (including locations in Georgia and South Carolina) and Georgia (Savannah), and (3) New Orleans LA (including locations in Mississippi, Alabama, Georgia and South Carolina.)

NORTHEAST – All five trains that enter North Carolina from the Northeast originate in New York City and pick up passengers in Newark NJ, Trenton NJ, Philadelphia PA, Wilmington DE, Baltimore MD, Washington DC, and Alexandria VA.

At Alexandria VA, one of the southbound trains – the **Crescent** – heads off to Manassas, Culpeper, Charlottesville, Lynchburg and Danville (all in VA) before entering North Carolina for stops in **Greensboro**, **High Point**, **Salisbury**, **Charlotte** and **Gastonia**. It then continues into South Carolina and through Georgia, Alabama and Mississippi on its way to New Orleans LA.

Two of the other southbound trains from the northeast – the **Silver Meteor** and the **Palmetto** – leave Alexandria VA, and make stops in Richmond VA and Petersburg VA before entering North Carolina for stops in **Rocky Mount**, **Wilson**, **Selma** (Palmetto only) and **Fayetteville**. The Silver Meteor then enters South Carolina and passes through Georgia and into Florida with Miami its final destination. The Palmetto also continues through South Carolina, but its final destination is Savannah GA.

The last two southbound trains from the northeast – the **Silver Star** and the **Carolinian** – also stop in **Rocky Mount** and **Wilson** after entering North Carolina but exit at **Selma** (where the Carolinian also stops) to head to **Raleigh** and **Cary** NC. At Cary, the Silver Star heads to **Southern Pines** and **Hamlet** before leaving North Carolina in the direction of Florida by way of South Carolina and Georgia. The Carolinian, however, departs Cary and first heads to **Durham**, after which it makes stops in **Burlington**, **Greensboro**, **High Point**, **Salisbury** and **Kannapolis** before its final destination **Charlotte**.

FLORIDA AND GEORGIA – Three daily trains enter North Carolina from the south – the **Silver Star**, the **Silver Meteor**, and the **Palmetto**. The **Silver Star** originates in Miami FL and makes many stops including Tampa, Orlando and Jacksonville (FL), Savannah GA and Columbia SC before entering North Carolina for stops in **Hamlet**, **Southern Pines**, **Cary**, **Raleigh** and **Rocky Mount**.

The **Silver Meteor** also originates in Miami and makes many stops including Orlando and Jacksonville (FL), Savannah GA, Charleston SC before entering North Carolina for stops in **Fayetteville** and **Rocky Mount**.

The **Palmetto** originates in Savannah GA and makes several stops in Charleston SC before entering North Carolina for stops in **Fayetteville**, **Selma**, **Wilson** and **Rocky Mount**.

NEW ORLEANS – The lone train that serves North Carolina from New Orleans is the **Crescent** which makes many station stops including Birmingham AL, Atlanta GA and Greenville SC before entering North Carolina for stops in **Gastonia**, **Charlotte**, **Salisbury**, **High Point** and **Greensboro** before heading through Virginia to New York.

HINT: Connections from other Amtrak trains serving New England, the Midwest and the West Coast can be made through New York City, Washington DC, and New Orleans (www.amtrak.com)

ARRIVING BY BUS

Many North Carolina cities have intercity bus service provided by Greyhound and its subsidiaries. Those cities that are served by both intercity bus and train include Charlotte, Greensboro, Durham, Raleigh, Rocky Mount, Wilson, Selma and Fayetteville. In Greensboro, Durham, Rocky Mount and Wilson, the intercity bus stations are adjacent to the train stations. In Charlotte, a taxicab is suggested for the two-mile trip from the Greyhound Station (601 W. Trade Street), although you could instead walk about 4 blocks to the Uptown Transportation Center and take Route 11 North Tryon to the train station (getting off at Tryon & Dalton).

In Raleigh, the Greyhound Station is one mile north of the Amtrak Station, an 8-block walk or a short taxicab ride. To get to the Selma Amtrak Station, the closest Greyhound Station is in Smithfield, 3.4 miles distant, so a taxicab is the only means.

Wilson is a connecting point for Greyhound buses from communities in northeastern North Carolina (including Greenville), and Rocky Mount is the same for communities in southeastern North Carolina (including Goldsboro, Kinston, Jacksonville and Wilmington.)

Greensboro and Durham serve as connecting points for communities in north central North Carolina, Greensboro for the northwest, Fayetteville for south central, and Charlotte for the southwest and far west.

For details on current Greyhound intercity bus services, go to: www.greyhound.com and for a map of Greyhound's system see:

www.discoverypass.com/maps/routemap_final_web.pdf

ARRIVING BY ROAD

Since it is conceivable that you plan on visiting friends or relatives who live in areas of North Carolina not served by passenger trains and will be offered a ride to the closest train station, this information is for you. For simplicity, only major highways that go through or near cities served by Amtrak passenger trains are included.

North Carolina is well-served by major multi-lane highways, both on the Interstate System and on the US System, and to a lesser extent on the NC System. For the latest version of the State Transportation Map, go to:

www.ncdot.org/travel/mappubs/statetransportationmap

If you approaching from the south, there is I-95 which goes by way of Fayetteville, Selma, Wilson and Rocky Mount, and I-85 which serves Gastonia, Charlotte, Kannapolis, Salisbury, High Point, Greensboro, Burlington and Durham.

From the west, I-40 enters the state from Tennessee, going by way of Asheville, Winston-Salem and Greensboro from which point it runs concurrently with I-85 until Durham when it branches off to Cary and Raleigh, and ultimately to Wilmington NC, its east coast end point.

From the north, there is I-95 which originates in Maine and enters North Carolina after going through Richmond and Petersburg (VA), then through North Carolina by way of Rocky Mount, Wilson, Selma and Fayetteville before heading into South Carolina on its course to Florida.

Also from the north, I-85 originates in Petersburg VA (at I-95) and then goes through North Carolina by way of Durham, Burlington, Greensboro, High Point, Salisbury, Kannapolis, Charlotte and Gastonia. Each of these interstate highways provides access to the remainder of North Carolina by way of US and NC-numbered routes.

WHAT NOW?

Now that you've arrived in North Carolina, you'll find out in Part 2 where you can go by train within North Carolina and, in Parts 3 and 4 what you can see and do with reasonable cost, convenience and comfort using each Amtrak Station as a base.

Part 2

TAKING THE TRAIN

There are currently sixteen active passenger train stations in North Carolina, although not all offer the same level of service or conveniences. Nine stations are located in the Piedmont corridor between Charlotte and Raleigh and have the most frequent service. These are Charlotte, Kannapolis, Salisbury, High Point, Greensboro, Burlington, Durham, Cary and Raleigh. The other seven stations are located on routes that take different paths through the state (Gastonia, Hamlet, Southern Pines, Selma, Fayetteville, Wilson and Rocky Mount) on their way to destinations in other states.

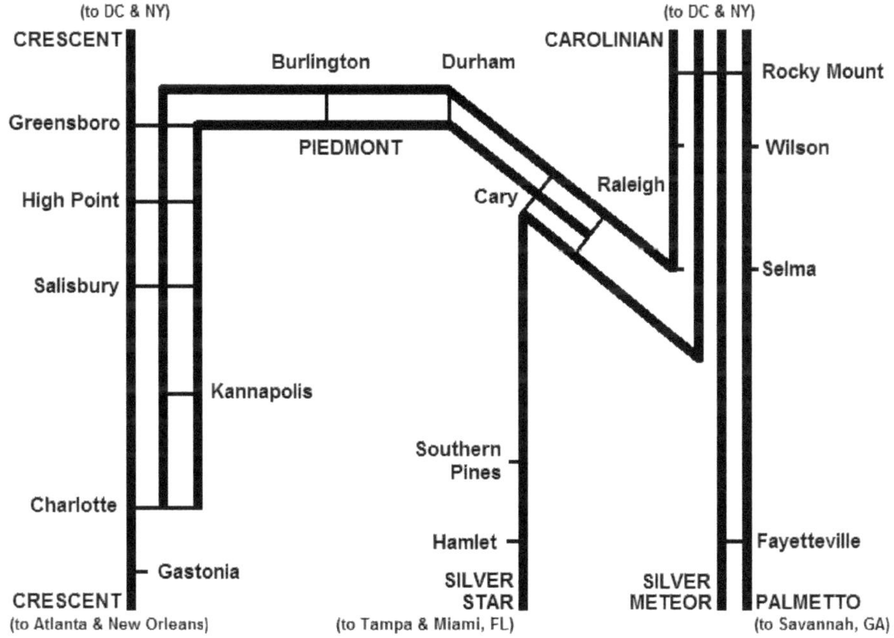

Passenger Train Routes in North Carolina

The Piedmont Corridor

The stations in the Piedmont Corridor are served by three daytime trains in each direction daily – the Carolinian (#79 south, #80 north), and two Piedmonts (#73 and #75 south, #74 and #76 north). As of publication date, the daily departure times are:

#80 READ DOWN	**#74** READ DOWN	**#76** READ DOWN	**PIEDMONT CORRIDOR STATION**	**#73** READ UP	**#75** READ UP	**#79** READ UP
7:00am	**12noon**	**5:15pm**	**Charlotte**	**9:55am**	**2:55pm**	**8:12pm**
7:25am	**12:25pm**	**5:40pm**	**Kannapolis**	**9:24am**	**2:24pm**	**7:41pm**
7:43am	**12:41pm**	**5:56pm**	**Salisbury**	**9:08am**	**2:08pm**	**7:24pm**
8:17am	**1:14pm**	**6:29pm**	**High Point**	**8:34am**	**1:34pm**	**6:48pm**
8:39am	**1:34pm**	**6:49pm**	**Greensboro**	**8:18am**	**1:18pm**	**6:32pm**
9:01am	**1:55pm**	**7:10pm**	**Burlington**	**7:53am**	**12:53pm**	**6:01pm**
9:42am	**2:33pm**	**7:48pm**	**Durham**	**7:17am**	**12:17pm**	**5:24pm**
10:02am	**2:53pm**	**8:08pm**	**Cary**	**6:57am**	**11:57am**	**5:03pm**
10:17am	**3:11pm**	**8:26pm**	**Raleigh**	**6:45am**	**11:45am**	**4:50pm**
11:00am			Selma			4:03pm
11:30am			Wilson			3:32pm
11:52am			Rocky Mt			3:13pm
8:43pm			*New York*			*7:05am*

Note that trains #79 and #80 (Carolinian) also serve three non-Piedmont Corridor stations, since the train runs between Charlotte, NC and New York, NY, via Raleigh

The Crescent Corridor

An additional night-time train serves four of the Piedmont Corridor stations (Charlotte, Salisbury, High Point and Greensboro) plus Gastonia. As of publication date, the daily departure times are:

Amtrak Crescent

Crescent #20 READ DOWN	**CRESCENT CORRIDOR STATION**	**Crescent #19** READ UP
2:15pm*	New York	1:46pm
12:39am	**Gastonia**	**3:12am**
1:21/1:46am**	**Charlotte**	**2:20/2:45am****
2:32am	**Salisbury**	**1:17am**
3:16am	**High Point**	**12:39am**
3:37am	**Greensboro**	**12:22am**
7:32pm	New Orleans	7:00am*

* previous day ** arrive/depart

Amtrak Silver Service and Palmetto

Three of Amtrak's long-distance trains make stops in North Carolina: the Silver Star and the Silver Meteor (between New York and Florida) and the Palmetto (between New York and Savannah, Georgia.) As of publication date, the daily trains' departure times are as follows:

Amtrak Silver Star, Silver Meteor and Palmetto

Silver Star **#92** READ DOWN	Silver Meteor **#98** READ DOWN	Palmetto **#90** READ DOWN	**SILVER SERVICE AND PALMETTO STATIONS**	Palmetto **#89** READ UP	Silver Meteor **#97** READ UP	Silver Star **#91** READ UP
*11:50am**	*8:20am**		*Miami*		*6:55pm*	*6:05pm***
		8:20am	*Savannah*	*9:03pm*		
6:29am			**Hamlet**			**11:21pm**
7:06am			**So. Pines**			**10:39pm**
8:15am			**Cary**			**9:27pm**
8:54am			**Raleigh**			**9:13pm**
	12:45am	**1:04pm**	**Fayetteville**	**3:44pm**	**1:34am**	
		1:51pm	**Selma**	**2:53pm**		
		2:23pm	**Wilson**	**2:22pm**		
10:15am	**2:17am**	**2:59pm**	**Rocky Mt**	**2:02pm**	**11:56pm**	**7:29pm**
7:18pm	*6:25pm*	*11:47pm*	*New York*	*6:15am*	*3:15pm*	*11:02am*

* previous day ** next day

You'll notice that some cities are listed in more than one of the previous three tables, so let's now take a look at the relative ease with which you can travel between North Carolina city pairs on a one-day excursion, and then ones which require an overnight stay.

One-Day Trips

In the Charlotte-to-Raleigh Piedmont Corridor, three trains in each direction mean that it is quite feasible for you to take an enjoyable one-day trip for work or pleasure to and from any of the nine cities.

The following two tables show the departure and return train numbers for Charlotte-to-Raleigh and for Raleigh-to-Charlotte one-day trips, and the approximate number of hours you will have to explore (or conduct business in) your destination during the day.

From Charlotte

Origin	Destination	Depart #	Return #	Visit Length*
Charlotte	Raleigh	80	79	6 hrs
→	Cary	80	79	7
→	Durham	80	79	7
→	Burlington	80 80 74	79 75 79	9 4 4
→	Greensboro	80 80 74	79 75 79	10 5 5
→	High Point	80 80 74	79 75 79	10 5 5
→	Salisbury	80 80 74	79 75 79	12 6 6
→	Kannapolis	80 80 74	79 75 79	12 7 5

* Only destination city visit lengths exceeding 2 hours are shown

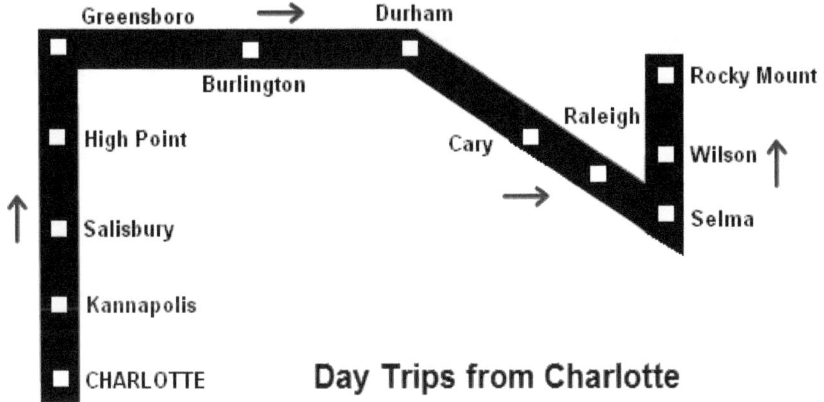

From Raleigh

Origin	Destination	Depart #	Return #	Visit Length*
Raleigh	Charlotte	73	76	7 hrs
→	Kannapolis	73 73 75	76 74 76	8 3 3
→	Salisbury	73 73 75	76 74 76	8 3 3
→	High Point	73 73 75	76 74 76	10 4 5
→	Greensboro	73 73 75	76 74 76	10 5 5
→	Burlington	73 73 75	76 74 76	11 6 6
→	Durham	73 73 75	76 74 76	12 7 7
→	Cary	73 73 75	76 74 76	13 8 8

* Only destination city visit lengths exceeding 2 hours are shown

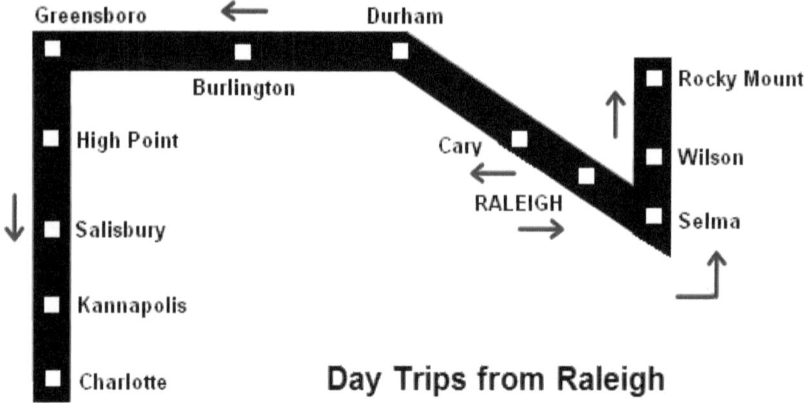

These are not the only one-day trips you can make, however. The northbound Silver Star (#92) and the northbound Carolinian (#80) enable a one-day excursion to be made from Cary or Raleigh to Rocky Mount, with the return on either the southbound Carolinian (#79) or the southbound Silver Star (#91). A one-day round-trip excursion between Hamlet or Southern Pines and Raleigh or Rocky Mount is also possible, but only on the Silver Star (#92 and #91), and therefore the day is long.

From Hamlet, Southern Pines, Cary and Raleigh on the Silver Star (#91/92) and Carolinian (#79/80)

Origin	Destination	Depart #	Return #	Visit Length	Day Length
Hamlet & So. Pines	Cary	92	91	13	17 hrs
→	Raleigh	92	91	12	17
→	Rocky Mt	92	91	9	17
Cary & Raleigh	Selma	80	79	5	7
→	Wilson	80	79	4	7
→	Rocky Mt	92 92 80	91 79 79	5 9 3	12 8 7

From Hamlet and Southern Pines on the Silver Star (#91/92) and Piedmont (#75/76)

Origin	Going Train 1	Change Trains	Going Train 2	Return Train 1	Change Trains	Return Train 2
Hamlet So. Pines	#92 d.6:29am d.7:06am	Cary: arrive 8:15am	#75 depart 11:57a	#76	Cary: arrive 8:08pm	#91 depart 9:27pm
Destination			**Arrive**	**Depart**		
Durham			12:17pm	7:48pm		
Burlington			12:53pm	7:10pm		
Greensboro			1:18pm	6:49pm		
High Point			1:34pm	6:29pm		
Salisbury			2:08pm	5:56pm		
Kannapolis			2:24pm	5:40pm		
Charlotte			2:55pm	5:15pm		

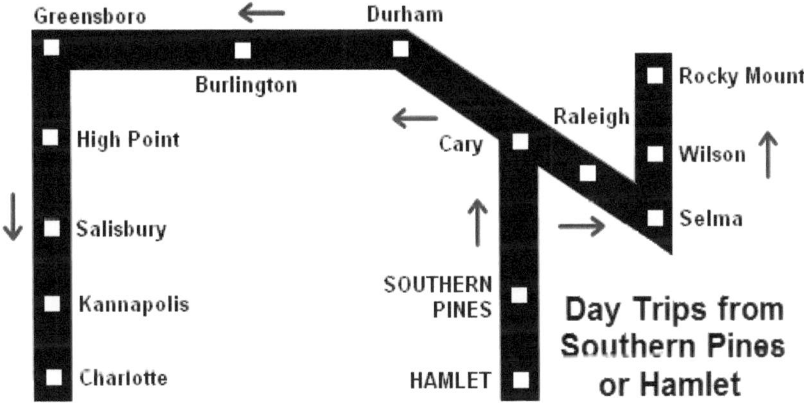

For completeness, the following table shows the possibility for one-day round trips by way of the Silver Meteor, the Palmetto, and the Carolinian:

From Fayetteville, Selma and Wilson
on the Palmetto (#89/90), Carolinian (#79/80) & Silver Meteor (#98)

Origin	Destination	Depart #	Return #	Visit Length	Day Length
Fayetteville	Selma	90	89	1 hrs	3 hrs
→	Rocky Mt	98	89	11	14
Selma	Wilson	80	79	4	5
→	Rocky Mt	80	79	4	5
Wilson	Rocky Mt	80	79	3	4

89/90 is Palmetto; 79/80 is Carolinian; 98 is northbound Silver Meteor

Note that all of the above one-day round trips are northbound-southbound in nature (between Fayetteville and Rocky Mount). No southbound-northbound one-day round trips are possible between Rocky Mount and Fayetteville.

Trips with an Overnight Stay

It almost goes without saying that any of one-day round trips can be turned into a trip with an overnight stay in the destination city. However, it is also already obvious from the included timetables that there are some cities for which the only way to visit is to stay overnight.

These are Gastonia, Hamlet, Southern Pines and Fayetteville from any direction, and Selma, Wilson and Rocky Mount from one direction or another. Since Fayetteville is the largest of these cities, let's look at that destination first.

• Fayetteville

Fayetteville is served during daylight hours by the Palmetto and during the night-time by the Silver Meteor. The Palmetto's connections with the Piedmont Corridor are Selma, Wilson and Rocky Mount (via the Carolinian), and the Silver Meteor's connection is Rocky Mount. Consequently a transfer from one train to another is going to be needed. Only daytime trains are shown since this trip can be made in two days with only one overnight stay in Fayetteville.

To Fayetteville

Origin	Going Train 1	Change Trains	Going Train 2	Return Train 1	Change Trains	Return Train 2
Hamlet, So. Pines, Cary & Raleigh	#92	Rocky Mount (4 hrs)*	#89	#90	Rocky Mount	#91
Charlotte, Kannapolis, Salisbury, High Point, Greensboro, Burlington, Durham, Cary & Raleigh	#80	Selma, Wilson or Rocky Mount (3-4 hrs)*	#89	#90	Selma, Wilson or Rocky Mount	#79
ARRIVE at Change Station & Destination		Rocky Mt 10:15am DAY 1	Rocky Mt 3:44pm DAY 1		Rocky Mt 2:59pm DAY 2	
DEPART Destination & Change Station				F'ville 1:04pm DAY 2	Rocky Mt	

* wait time between trains

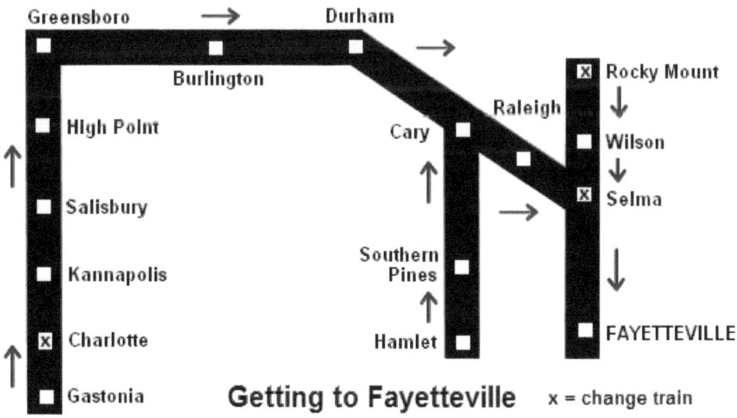

Getting to Fayetteville

• Southern Pines and Hamlet

The only train that serves these two communities is the Silver Star for which either Cary or Raleigh would be the connecting point with Piedmont Corridor service (Piedmont and Carolinian trains), and Rocky Mount for a connection from Fayetteville (the Palmetto train.)

Since you will arrive in Southern Pines or Hamlet in late evening on Day 1, in order to sightsee in either of these two communities during daylight hours on Day 2, your return will need be no earlier than Day 3 (two nights stay.)

To Southern Pines and Hamlet

Origin	Going Train 1	Change Trains	Going Train 2	Return Train 1	Change Trains	Return Train 2
Charlotte, Kannapolis, Salisbury, High Point, Greensboro, Burlington, Durham	#76 DAY 1	Cary DAY 1	#91 DAY 1	#92 DAY 3	Cary DAY 3	#75 DAY 3
Rocky Mt	#91 DAY 1	No Change	-	#92 DAY 3	No Change	-
Wilson & Selma	#79 DAY 1	Cary	#91 DAY 1	#92 DAY 3	Cary	#80 DAY 3
Fayetteville	#90 DAY 1	Rocky Mount	#91 DAY 1	#92 DAY 3	Rocky Mount	#89 DAY 3

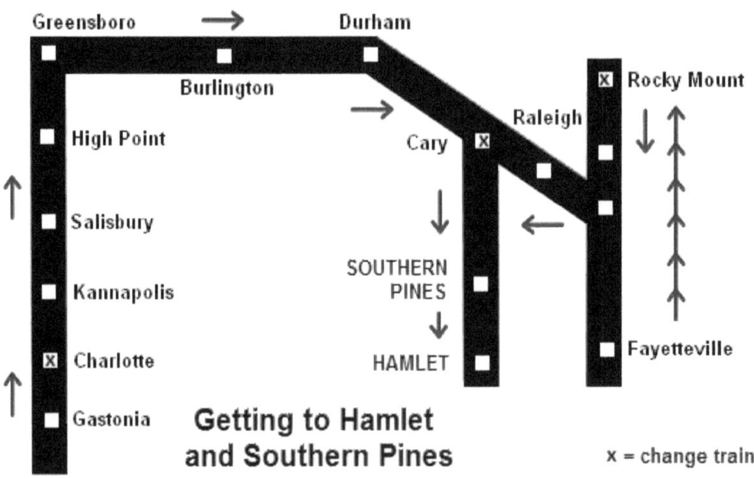

Getting to Hamlet and Southern Pines

• Gastonia

Because it is only served by one train in each direction daily (and in the middle of the night too), Gastonia is not going to be high on your priority list, unless you are determined to ride every mile of passenger train service in North Carolina. The table below shows three options, depending on where you are starting your trip. Option A involves the southbound Carolinian to Charlotte from any of the cities in the Piedmont Corridor plus Selma, Wilson and Rocky Mount, and then a change (after a long wait) to the southbound Crescent. Option 2 involves only the southbound Crescent but is limited to boarding at Greensboro, High Point, Salisbury or Charlotte. Option 3 is for when your trip originates in Hamlet or Southern Pines, and Option 4 is for a Fayetteville origination.

To Gastonia

Origin	Going Train 1	Change Trains	Going Train 2	Return Train 1	Change Trains	Return Train 2
OPTION A Piedmont Corridor Cities, plus Selma, Wilson & Rocky Mt	#79 DAY 1	Charlotte DAY 1 (4 hrs)*	#19 DAY 2 (night)	#20 DAY 3 (night)	Charlotte DAY 3 (5 hrs)*	#80 DAY 3
OPTION B Greensboro, High Point, Salisbury, Charlotte	#19 DAY 1 (night)	No Change	-	#20 DAY 3 (night)	No Change	-
OPTION C Hamlet & So. Pines	#92	Cary or Raleigh (9 hrs)*	#79 & #19	#20 & #80	Cary or Raleigh (11 hrs)*	#91
OPTION D Fayetteville	#90	Selma, Wilson or Rocky Mt	#79 & #19	#20 & #80	Selma, Wilson or Rocky Mt	#91

#79/80 – Carolinian; #19/20 – Crescent; * wait time between trains

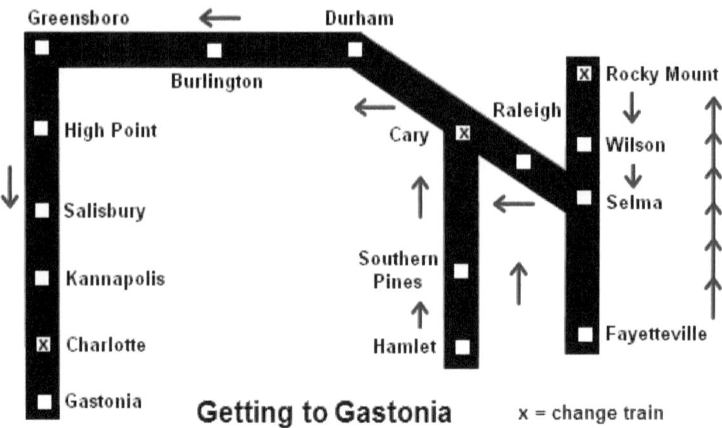

Special Event Stops

Each year, two stops are made by trains in North Carolina to accommodate special events. One is the State Fair in Raleigh which runs for ten days about the third week in October, and the other is the one-day Barbecue Festival in Lexington (between High Point and Salisbury.) For the State Fair, the stop is at the intersection of Hillsborough St and Blue Ridge Rd. The northbound Carolinian (#80) from Charlotte and stations in-between drops off passenger at 10:17am, and the southbound Carolinian (#79) picks up returning passengers at 4:50pm. For the Lexington Barbecue Festival (the Saturday of the last full weekend of October each year), all trains in the Piedmont Corridor make a special stop in downtown Lexington. Precise information on the train time tables for these two special stops will be posted in advance at www.bytrain.org

Train and Bus Trips

If you want to travel to a North Carolina city not served by an Amtrak train, you do have another option – the intercity bus. As you see from the diagram on page 25, intercity buses operated by Greyhound and Coach America will enable you to visit some other important cities like Asheville and Wilmington, as well as many other communities.

These bus services originate in cities with train service, so changing from the train to the bus is convenient in many instances. For complete information on intercity bus services and timetables, go to Greyhound's website at www.greyhound.com, and Coach America's website at www.coachamerica.com.

The only intercity bus service that officially connects with Amtrak train service (i.e., waits until trains have arrived and departed) is the Winston-Salem NC Amtrak Connector which meets the Carolinian and Piedmont trains at High Point. It runs to and from Winston-Salem with an intermediate stop at Winston-Salem State University.

The Cost of Tickets

This book would be incomplete if there were no mention of the passenger fares for riding trains and buses. However, since ticket prices are established by Amtrak and can vary from one season to season, are discounted for certain categories of travelers, and may be available for special promotions, all I can do is inform you of the lowest current un-discounted one-way adult fares (purchased at least one day in advance), and the various conditions that might produce even lower fares.

PIEDMONT CORRIDOR FARES(adult, one-way, undiscounted, in US $)

BETWEEN	CYN	CLT	DNC	GRO	HPT	KAN	RGH	SAL
BNC	9.50	24.50	5.50	7.00	8.00	22.00	9.00	19.00
CYN	-	32.50	5.50	12.50	18.00	30.00	5.50	25.00
CLT		-	25.50	17.50	15.00	5.50	27.50	9.50
DNC			-	11.50	17.50	28.50	6.00	23.50
GRO				-	5.50	15.00	12.50	13.00
HPT					-	11.50	15.00	9.50
KAN						-	25.50	5.50
RGH							-	28.00

As of April 2012

OTHER FARES (adult, one-way, undiscounted, in US $)

BETWEEN	CLT	RGH	SSM	FAY	WLN	RMT	SOP	HAM
GAS	7.50c1	35.00x	43.00x	70.50xw	49.50x	53.50x	59.00xr	66.00xr
CLT	-	27.50	35.50	63.00w	42.00	46.00	52.00r	58.50r
RGH		-	7.00	32.00w	11.00	18.00	24.00s	31.00s
SSM			-	10.00	7.00	10.00	28.00r	35.00r
FAY				-	21.00p	30.00m 23.00p	56.00w	61.00w
WLN					-	7.00	35.00r	40.00r
RMT						-	38.00s	42.00s
SOP							-	15.00s

As of April 2012
c=Crescent ; x=change in CLT; xw=change in CLT & WLN; w=change in WLN
xr=change in CLT and RGH; r=change in RGH; s=Silver Star; m=Silver Meteor
p=Palmetto

When first confronted with ticket fares, many potential train riders compare the ticket cost to the cost of filling their car with fuel and conclude that train travel is more expensive. Remember, the train ticket is your total transportation cost (except for local travel) for that trip, whereas your fuel cost is only one of many costs of owning and driving a car. When you take the cost of the train ticket and divide it by the miles you travel, you will see that the cost is quite reasonable. For example, the one-way distance (by road) between Raleigh and Charlotte is 143 miles and the adult train ticket costs $27.50, which is 19.2 cents per mile, much less than the IRS 2012 Business Mileage rate of 55.5 cents. Also, remember for that cost you will have a relaxing and productive trip during which you can read a book, listen to music or watch a movie (earphones, please!), talk to your companion or a complete stranger, work on your laptop or tablet, talk (quietly) on your phone – everything that you cannot or should not do when you are driving on the highway.

Reductions to the above fares are available as follows:

Children (aged 2-15) half-price; infants under 2 ride free; **Seniors** aged 62 and above receive 15% off basic fare; does not apply to upgrades to business class or accommodations; **AAA Members** receive 10% discount off basic fare; does not apply to upgrades to business class or accommodations (3 days advance purchase required) **Active Duty US Military** personnel, their spouses and their dependents, are eligible to receive a 10% discount off most Amtrak rail fares. **NARP Members**, **Student Advantage Card**, **International Student Identity Card** and **Veterans Advantage** Members may also receive discounts.

For the latest information on discounts, go to www.amtrak.com and click on the "Deals" tab, and "Passenger Discounts" in the menu.

Renting a Bicycle

If you have your own bicycle, note that you may take it on any of the Piedmont trains #73, 74, 75 & 76 (it goes in a rack in the baggage car, and although there is no charge, you will need to include your bicycle when you make your reservation. Your transportation in any of the Piedmont Corridor cities is thus solved.

Alternatively, you can rent a bicycle at your destination. The Bicycle & Pedestrian Transportation Division of the NC Department of Transportation maintains a list of bicycle shops across the state; see www.ncdot.gov/bikeped/bicycle/bikeshops/ Most of the shops contacted do have a few bicycles for rent, but it would be wise to contact the them in advance to ensure that one will be available when you want it, and pay attention to the shops' hours of operation.

Most towns and cities have signed or at least mapped bicycle routes and trails; these you may view also at www.ncdot.gov/bikeped/ as well as pick up maps at travel information offices.

Summary

You should now be sufficiently knowledgeable to start planning your train trip in North Carolina. Where to go and what to see and how to get around without a car are the next decisions to make. The attractions you won't want to miss are listed in Part 3, as are links to local travel and tourism bureaus. Finally, in Part 4 are some ideas that may satisfy your particular interests – I've called them "theme trips."

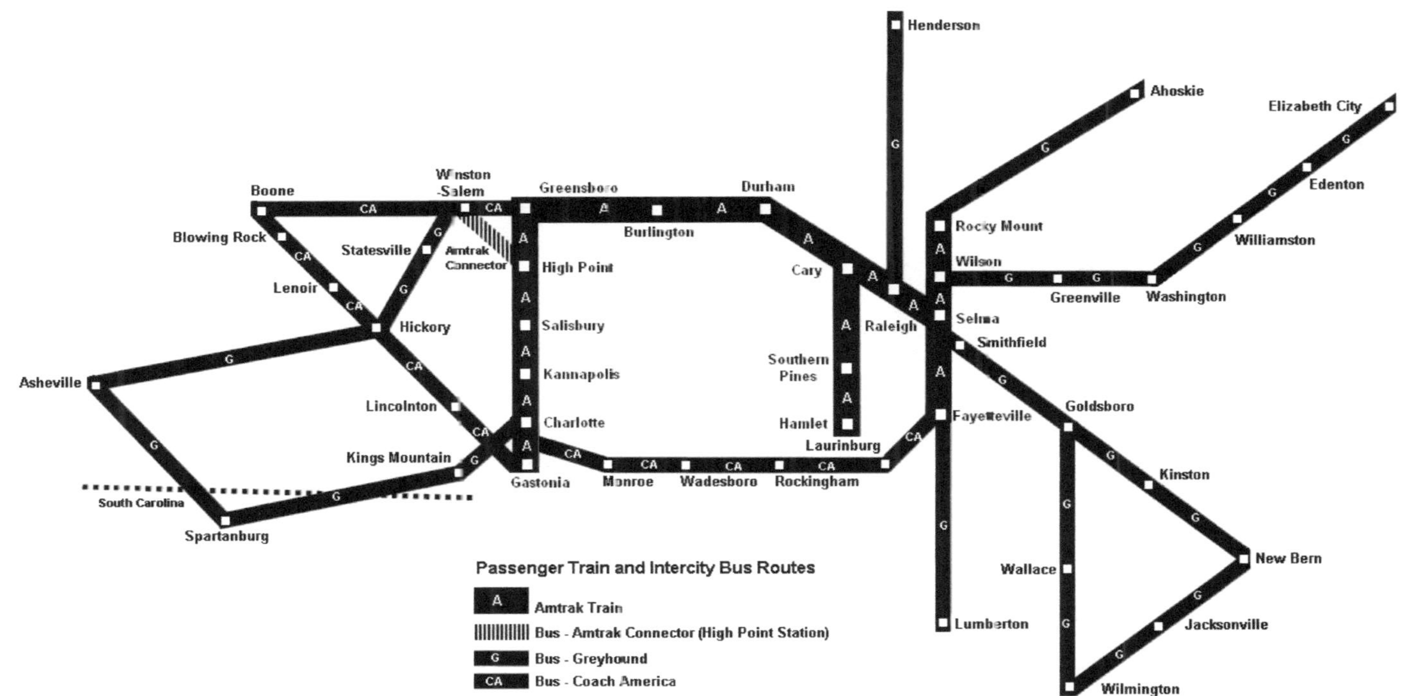
Henderson
Ahoskie
Elizabeth City
Edenton
Williamston
Boone
Winston -Salem
Greensboro
Durham
Blowing Rock
Statesville
Amtrak Connector
Burlington
Rocky Mount
Wilson
High Point
Cary
Greenville
Washington
Lenoir
Hickory
Salisbury
Raleigh
Selma
Smithfield
Asheville
Kannapolis
Southern Pines
Lincolnton
Charlotte
Hamlet
Fayetteville
Goldsboro
Laurinburg
Kings Mountain
Gastonia
Monroe
Wadesboro
Rockingham
Kinston
South Carolina
Spartanburg
New Bern
Wallace
Lumberton
Jacksonville
Wilmington
Passenger Train and Intercity Bus Routes
Amtrak Train
Bus - Amtrak Connector (High Point Station)
Bus - Greyhound
Bus - Coach America

Symbols used in City Maps

KANNAPOLIS AMTRAK STATION, author photo

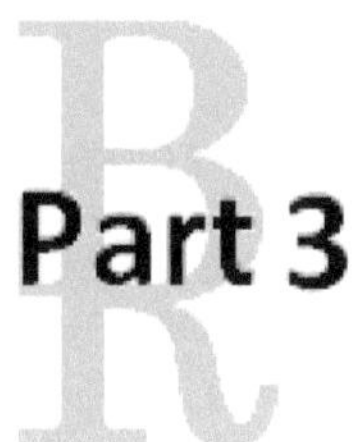

Part 3

WHAT TO SEE AND DO

We'll now take a look, in alphabetical order, at each North Carolina city served by Amtrak passenger trains (plus Winston-Salem) and explore the various attractions, learn what local transportation is available, where you can eat, where you can stay if you're planning an overnight trip, and where you can get additional information before and during your trip. Note that food establishments are only listed for the smaller cities where opportunities are less plentiful. Also note that not all museums are open on Mondays, so you need to check in advance for operating days and hours. Ideas for special theme trips to each city are described in Part 4.

BURLINGTON (pop. 49,963), Alamance County, Area Code: 336
Incorporated 1893; previous called "Company Shops" for NC Railroad Company locomotive repair facility located there in 1851
Amtrak Station (BNC): 101 N. Main St, Tel: 336-570-7043
Buses: none
City website: www.burlingtonnc.gov

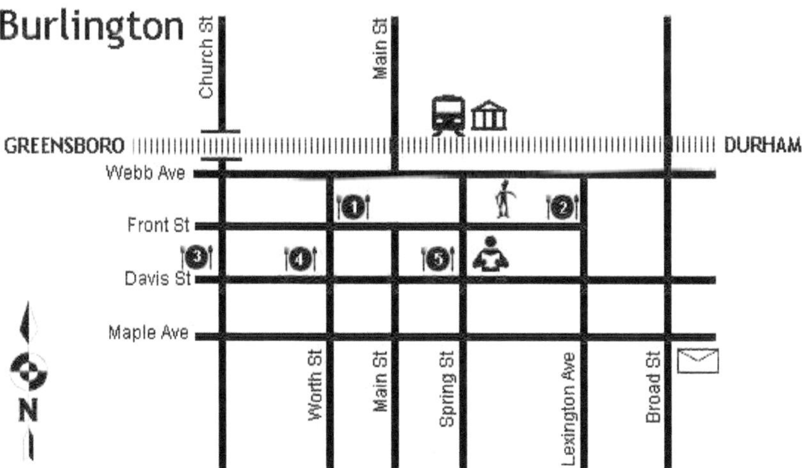

• **ATTRACTIONS** (downtown unless noted)
1910 Dentzel Menagerie Carousel, Burlington City Park (S. Main & S. Church); **Whistlestop Exhibit at Company Shops Station** (Amtrak Station); **Paramount Theatre**, 128 E. Front St (walk); **Burlington Downtown Corporation**, Webb Ave downtown (located in **Historic Depot**); **Caboose Museum** (next to Historic Depot,

Sat 1-4 only)

- **WALKING TOUR**
  www.burlingtondowntown.com/maps.htm (click on "Alamance Walks" for brochure)
- **FOOD** (downtown)
  Danny's Café (1), 110 W. Front St (walk); **Company Shops Market (2)**, 268 E. Front St (walk); **Subway (3)**, 260 W. Davis St (walk); **Zack's (4)**, 201 W. Davis St (walk), **Perk-O-Later (5)**, 132 E. Davis St (walk)
- **LODGING** (out of downtown)
  BarberShop Guest House (B&B), 2440 Glencoe St (taxi), www.rockworthhouse.com; **Courtyard by Marriott**, 3141 Wilson Dr (taxi) www.marriott.com/gsobr
- **OTHER** (downtown)
  Post Office, 405 E. Maple Ave (walk); **Public Library**, 342 S. Spring St (walk); **Burlington/Alamance Convention & Visitors Bureau** (CVB) 610 S. Lexington (walk); **Courthouse,** 212 W. Elm St, Graham; **Police**, 267 W. Front St
- **NEWSPAPER**
  Times-News, www.thetimesnews.com

AMTRAK'S CAROLINIAN AT BURLINGTON STATION, author photo

CARY (pop. 135,234), Wake County, Area Codes: 919, 984

Incorporated 1871 as "Carey"; originally known as "Page's Tavern", and after railroad built as Page's Siding; spelling changed to "Cary" around 1899
Amtrak Station (CYN): 211 N. Academy St, Tel: (919) 462-6434
Buses: C/Tran (in Amtrak Station)
C/Tran Route Map:
www.townofcary.org/Assets/Planning+Department/Planning+Department+PDFs/ctran/busschedules.pdf
Town website: www.townofcary.org

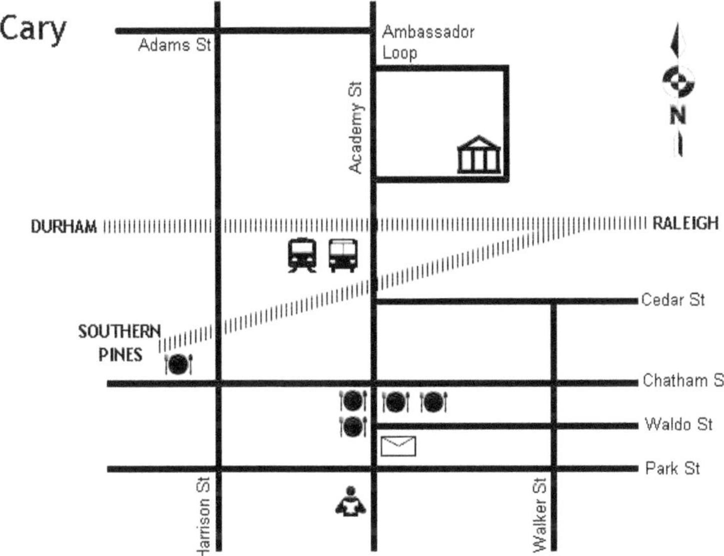

- **ATTRACTIONS** (downtown unless noted)
  Page-Walker Arts & History Center, 119 Ambassador Loop; **Cary Heritage Museum** (same address);
- **WALKING TOUR**
  http://www.townofcary.org/Departments/Planning_Department.htm (click on "Maps" and then "Bike & Hike Map")
- **FOOD** (downtown)
  Ashworth Drugs (soda fountain), 105 W. Chatham St; **Chatham Street Café**, 140 E. Chatham St; **Havana Grill**, 404 W. Chatham St; **Klara's Restaurant**, 200 S. Academy St; **Once In A Blue Moon Bakery**, 115 W. Chatham St; **Serendipity Gourmet Deli**, 118 S. Academy St; **Spirits Pub & Grub**, 710 E. Chatham St; **Taipei 101**, 121 E. Chatham St; **The Chefs of India**, 748 E. Chatham St; **Udupi Café**, 590 E. Chatham St;
- **LODGING** (out of downtown)
  Best Western, 1722 Walnut St; **Comfort Suites**, 350 Asheville Ave; **Courtyard by Marriott**, 102 Edinburgh Dr S; **Embassy Suites**, 201 Harrison Oaks Blvd; for others see www.visitraleigh.com/
- **OTHER** (downtown)

Public Library, 310 S. Academy St; **Post Office**, 205 S. Academy St; **Ashworth Drugs**, 105 W. Chatham St; **Police**, 120 Wilkinson Ave;

- **NEWSPAPER**

  Cary News, www.carynews.com

PAGE-WALKER ARTS & HISTORY CENTER, author photo

CHARLOTTE (pop. 731,424), Mecklenburg County, Area Codes: 704, 980

Incorporated 1768, named for Charlotte, queen of England's George III
Amtrak Station (CLT): 1914 N. Tryon St, Tel: (704) 376-4416
Buses: CATS, LYNX (light rail) & Greyhound
CATS Route Maps:
www.charmeck.org/city/charlotte/cats/Bus/maps/Pages/default.aspx
City website: www.charmeck.org

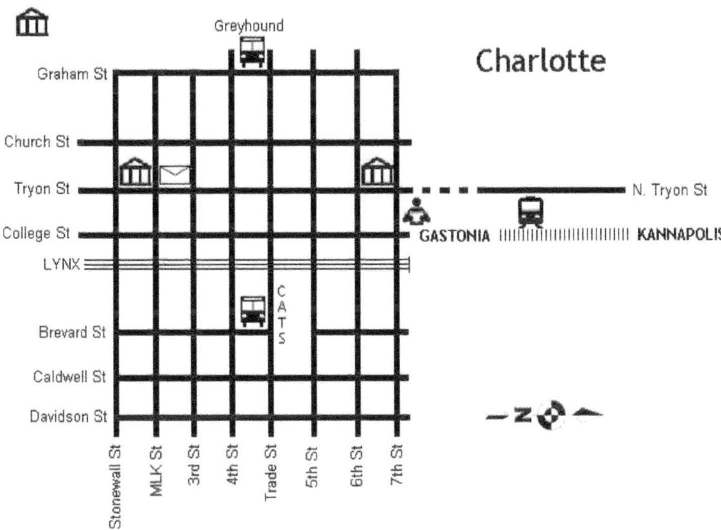

- **ATTRACTIONS** (center city, aka "uptown" unless noted)
  Discovery Place, 201 N. Tryon St; Mint Museum Uptown, 500 S. Tryon St; **Museum of the New South**, 200 E. Seventh St; **LYNX Light Rail**, Trade St & College St; **NASCAR Hall of Fame**, 400 E. Martin Luther King, Jr. Blvd; **Charlotte Trolley Powerhouse Museum**, 1507 Camden Rd (LYNX Bland St Station); **Carolinas Aviation Museum**, 4672 First Flight Dr (CLT Airport);
- **WALKING TOUR**
  http://www.artsandscience.org/public-art-program (click on "Public Art Walking Tour")
- **FOOD**
  Amtrak Station, snack and drink machines only;
  Center City, **Subway**, 101 N. Tryon St/201 N. Tryon St/301 S. Tryon St/310 E. Trade St /135 Brevard Ct/626 N. Graham; **Chick-Fil-A**, 101 S. Tryon St; **Jason's Deli**, 210 E. Trade St; **Bojangles**, 501 S. College St; **Vida Mexican Kitchen y Cantina**, 210 E. Trade St
- **LODGING** (center city)
  Lodging Guide, www.charlottesgotalot.com/default.asp?charlotte=54
- **OTHER** (center city)
  Post Office, 300 S. Tryon St; **Public Library**, 300 E. 7th St; **Courthouse**, 832 E. Fourth St; **Police**, 119 E. 7th St
- **NEWSPAPER**
  Charlotte Observer, www.charlotteobserver.com

DURHAM (pop. 228,330), Durham County; Area Code: 919

Incorporated 1866, originally named "Durhamsville" after Dr. Bartlett Snipes Durham who donated the land for the railroad station, changed to "Durham" in 1855
Amtrak Station (DNC): 601 W. Main St; Tel:
Buses: DATA, Triangle Transit , Greyhound
DATA Route Map: http://data.durhamnc.gov/pdf/ride_guide_map.pdf
City website: www.durhamnc.gov

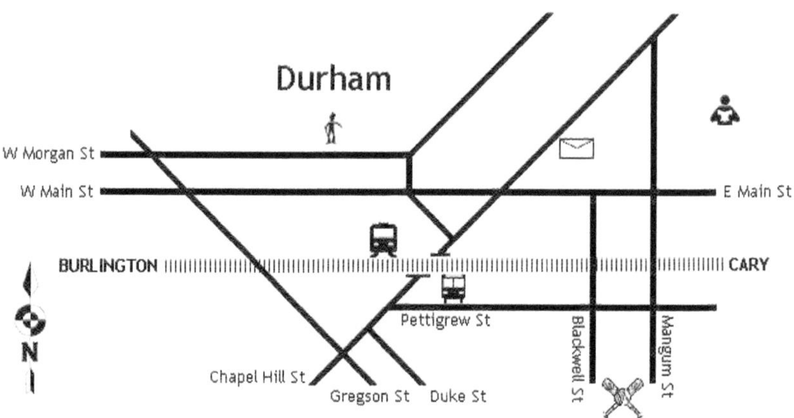

- **ATTRACTIONS** (downtown unless noted)
  Durham Bulls, 409 Blackwell St; **Durham Performing Arts Center (DPAC)**, 123 Vivian St; **Carolina Theatre**, 309 W. Morgan St; **Visitor Information**, 101 E. Morgan St; **American Tobacco**, 318 Blackwell St; **Brightleaf Square**, Gregson St at W. Main St; also see Part 4
- **WALKING TOUR**
  http://www.preservationdurham.org/events/weekly_walking.html (free, Apr-Oct, 2nd, 3rd & 4th Sa, 10am, 90 min); Downtown Guide and Walking Tour, www.durham-nc.com/resources/pdf/tourmap_walk.pdf
- **FOOD** (downtown)
  Dining Guide www.durham-nc.com/dining/
- **LODGING** (downtown)
  Lodging Guide www.durham-nc.com/hotels-inns/
- **OTHER** (downtown)
  Post Office, 323 E. Chapel Hill St; **Public Library**, 300 N. Roxboro St; **Courthouse**, 200 E. Main St; **Police**, 505 W. Chapel Hill St;
- **NEWSPAPER**
  Herald-Sun, www.heraldsun.com

FAYETTEVILLE (pop. 200,564), Cumberland County; Area Code 910
Incorporated 1762 as "Campbellton" after Farquhard Campbell; changed to "Fayetteville" in 1783 in honor of Marquis de Lafayette
Amtrak Station (FAY): 472 Hay St; Tel. 910-483-2658
Buses: FAST, Greyhound
FAST Route Map: www.ridefast.net/routes.aspx
City website: www.cityoffayetteville.org

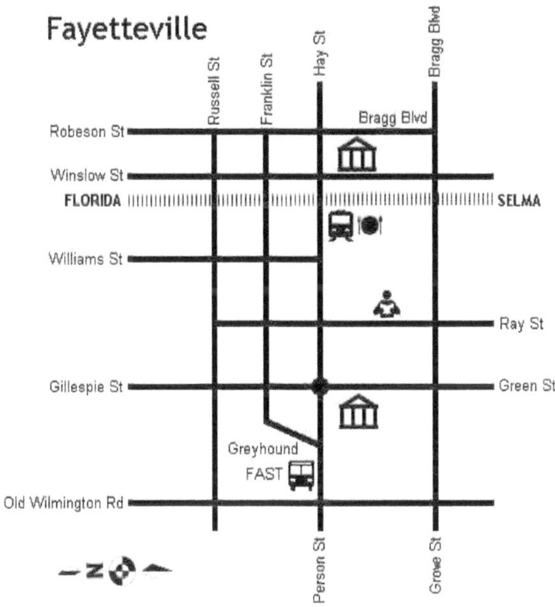

- **ATTRACTIONS** (downtown unless noted)
  Airborne & Special Operations Museum, 100 Bragg Blvd; **Fascinate-U Children's Museum**, 116 Green St; **Museum of the Cape Fear**, 801 Arsenal Ave; **1832 Market House**, Hay, Gillespie, Person & Green Sts; St. Joseph's Episcopal Church, 509 Ramsey St; **Fayetteville Transportation Museum** (former Cape Fear & Yadkin Valley Railroad Depot), 325 Franklin St; **82nd Airborne Division War Memorial Museum**, Ardennes & Gela Sts (Fort Bragg); **Fayetteville Independent Light Infantry Armory & Museum**, 210 Burgess St; **JFK Special Warfare Museum**, Ardennes & Marion Sts (Fort Bragg); **Fayetteville State University Planetarium**, 1200 Murchison Rd; **Visitor Information**, 245 Person St
- **FOOD** (downtown)
  Subway, 472 Hay St (in Amtrak Station); for others in central Fayetteville, see www.visitfayettevillenc.com/restaurants/search/zone/id/11/Central+Fayetteville
- **LODGING**
  See www.visitfayettevillenc.com/accommodations/search/results/sort/name
- **OTHER** (downtown)
  Post Office, 301 Green St; **Public Library**, 300 Maiden Lane; **Courthouse**, 117 Dick St; **Police**, 467 Hay St;

• **NEWSPAPER**
Fayetteville Observer, www.fayobserver.com

AIRBORNE & SPECIAL OPERATIONS MUSEUM, FAYETTEVILLE, author photo

GASTONIA (pop. 71,741), Gaston County; Area Code: 704
Incorporated 1877, named after county in which located, which was named after William Gaston, a member of the US Congress and State Supreme Court Judge
Amtrak Station (GAS): 350 Hancock St; Tel: 800-872-7245 (800-USA-RAIL)
Buses: GTS (Gastonia Transit System), Greyhound & Coach America
GTS Route Map:
www.cityofgastonia.com/city_serv/fleet/_pdf%20files/TransitMapMarch2012.pdf
City website: www.cityofgastonia.com

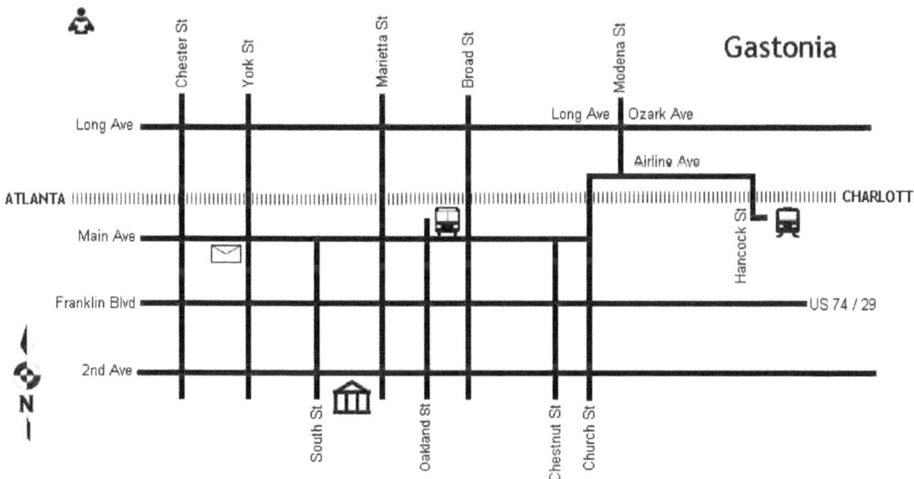

• **ATTRACTIONS** (downtown unless noted)
American Military Museum, 109 W. 2nd St; **Visitor Information**, 620 N. Main St (Belmont) or www.visitgaston.org/

• **FOOD** (downtown)
Subway, 250 E. Garrison St; also see www.visitgaston.org/gaston-county-dining

• **LODGING** (out of downtown)
Lodging Guide, www.visitgaston.org/gaston-county-hotels

• **OTHER** (downtown)
Post Office, 301 W. Main Ave; **Public Library**, 913 Pryor St; **Courthouse**, 325 N. Marietta St; **Police**, 200 E. Long Ave;

• **NEWSPAPER**
Gaston Gazette, www.gastongazette.com

GREENSBORO (pop. 269,666), Guilford County; Area Code: 336
Incorporated 1810, named for General Nathanael Greene, American leader at Battle of Guilford Courthouse, 1781
Amtrak Station (GRO): 236 E. Washington St; Tel: 336-272-6755
Buses: GTA, PART & Greyhound
GTA Route Map: www.greensboro-nc.gov/index.aspx?page=2185
City website: www.greensboro-nc.gov

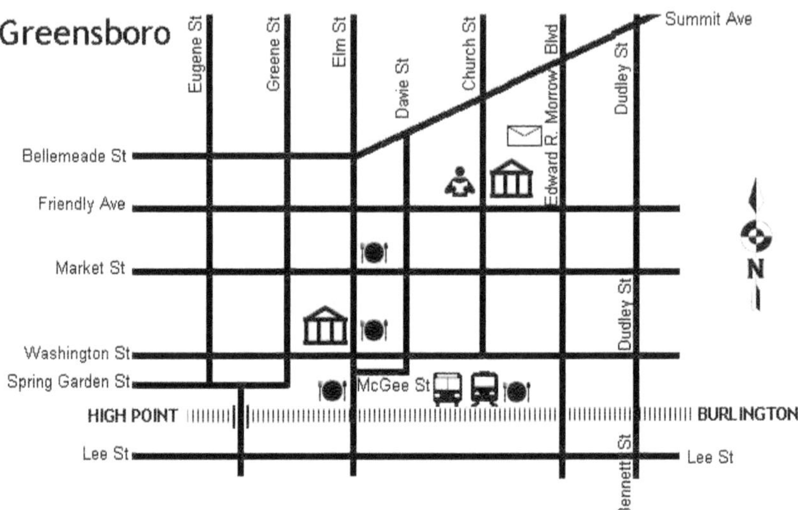

- **ATTRACTIONS** (downtown unless noted)
  International Civil Rights Center & Museum, 134 S. Elm St; **Greensboro Historical Museum**, 130 Summit Ave; **Greensboro Children's Museum**, 220 N. Church St; **Blandwood Mansion**, 447 W. Washington St; **Cultural Center**, 200 N. Davie St; **ACC Hall of Champions** (Greensboro Coliseum), 1921 W. Lee St
- **FOOD** (downtown)
  Subway, 106 N. Elm St; also see www.visitgreensboronc.com/dining
- **LODGING** (downtown unless noted)
  Lodging Guide, www.visitgreensboronc.com/accommodations
- **OTHER** (downtown)
  Post Office, 201 N. Edward R. Murrow Blvd; **Public Library**, 219 N. Church St; **Courthouse**, 201 S. Eugene St; **Police**, 300 W. Washington St;
- **NEWSPAPER**
  News and Record, www.news-record.com

HAMLET (pop. 6,495), Richmond County; Area Code: 910
Incorporated 1897, named for the word that then described its size; important railroad center with maintenance shops
Amtrak Station (HAM): 2 Main St; Tel: 800-872-7245 (800-USA-RAIL)
Buses: none
City website: www.hamletnc.us

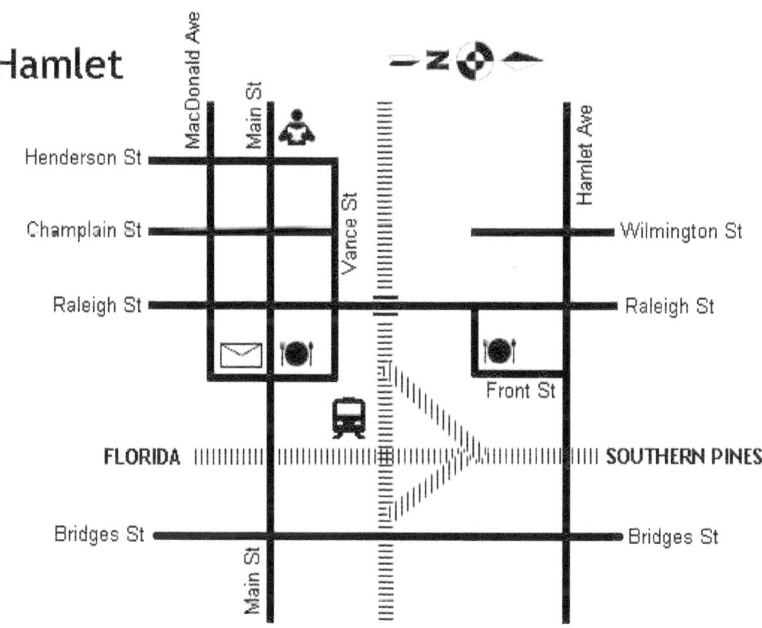

- **ATTRACTIONS** (downtown unless noted)
  Hamlet Railroad Depot (Amtrak Station); **Depot Museum** (Amtrak Station, Sa/Su only); **NC Railroad Museum & Hall of Fame**, 120 Spring St (Sa 11-4/Su 1-4 only or by appointment)
- **FOOD** (downtown)
  Main Street Café, 38 W. Main St (closed Su/M); **Seaboard Station Restaurant**, 12 Charlotte St (lunch); **Subway**, 819 W. Hamlet Ave; **Main St Soda Shop**, 34 W. Main St; **Burger King**, 542 W. Hamlet Ave; **Hardees**, 701 W. Hamlet Ave;
- **LODGING** (out of downtown)
  Lodging Guide, www.visitrichmondcounty.com/accommodations.html
- **OTHER** (downtown)
  Post Office, Main & Lackey; **Public Library**, 302 W. Main St; **Police**, 201 Main St;
- **NEWSPAPER**
  Richmond County Daily Journal, www.yourdailyjournal.com

HIGH POINT (pop. 104,371), Guilford County; Area Code: 336
Incorporated 1859, named for being the highest point (elevation 940') on North Carolina Railroad; intersection of railroad and Fayetteville & Western Plank Road
Amtrak Station (HPT): 100 W. High Ave; Tel: 336-884-0878
Buses: Hi tran, PART & Greyhound
Hi tran Route Maps: www.high-point.net/hi-tran/routes.cfm
City website: www.high-point.net

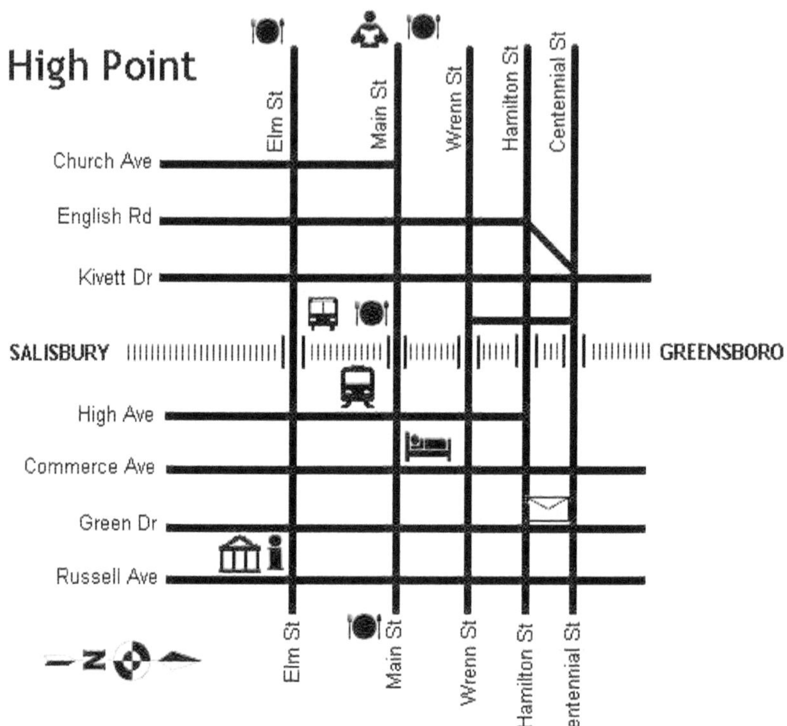

- **ATTRACTIONS** (downtown unless noted)
  Doll & Miniature Museum, 101 W. Green Dr; **High Point Museum**, 1859 E. Lexington St; Visitor Information, 300 S. Main St; **Furniture Market**, www.highpointmarket.org, also see www.highpoint.org
- **FOOD** (downtown)
  Subway, 200 Westwood Ave; also see http://highpoint.org/cvb/cat/category/restaurants/
- **LODGING** (downtown, unless noted)
  Best Western High Point, 135 S. Main St (across from Amtrak Station); also see http://highpoint.org/cvb/cat/category/accommodations/
- **OTHER** (downtown)
  Post Office, 315 E. Green Dr; **Public Library**, 901 N. Main St; **Police**, 1009 Leonard Ave
- **NEWSPAPER**
  High Point Enterprise, www.hpe.com

KANNAPOLIS (pop. 42,625), Cabarrus County; Area Code: 704
Incorporated 1982, previously was an unincorporated company (Cannon Mills) town
Amtrak Station (**KAN**): 201 S. Main St; Tel: 704-932-1591
Buses: Rider & Greyhound
Rider Route Maps: http://030c993.netsolhost.com/MapsSchedules/SystemMap.aspx
City websites: www.cityofkannapolis.com & www.concordnc.gov

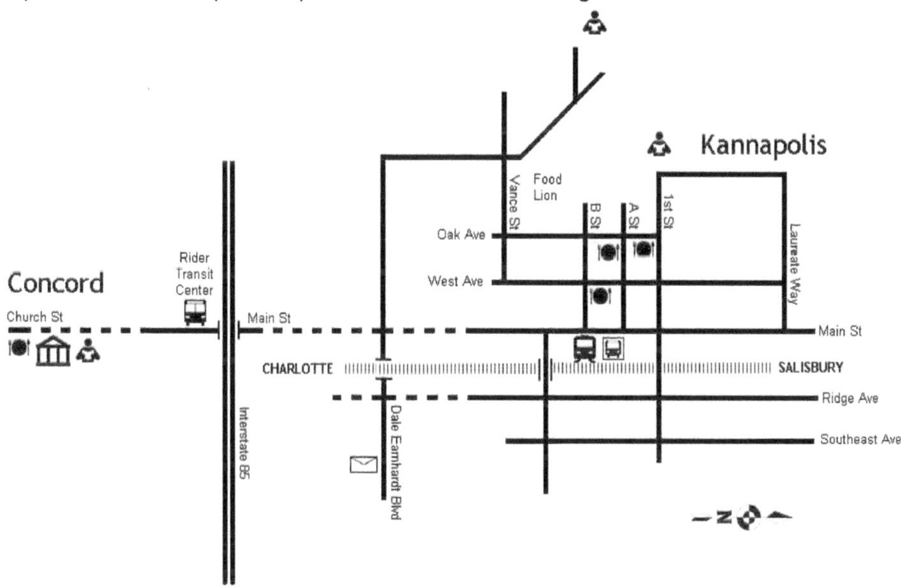

- **ATTRACTIONS** (downtown unless noted)
  Dale Earnhardt Memorial Garden, across Main St from Amtrak Station; **NC Music Hall of Fame**, W. A St; **NC Research Campus**, N. Main St; www.visitcabarrus.com
- **FOOD** (downtown)
  Restaurant 46, W. 1st Ave; **Sunshine's Asian Cuisine**, 215 W. A St; also see www.visitcabarrus.com
- **LODGING** (out of downtown)
  Lodging Guide, www.visitcabarrus.com; many hotels reachable by Rider bus
- **OTHER** (downtown)
  Post Office, 1040 Dale Earnhardt Blvd (Kannapolis) & 66 McCachern Blvd SE (Concord); **Public Library**, 850 Mountain St (Kannapolis) & 27 Union St N (Concord); **Courthouse** (Concord); **Police**, 314 S. Main St (Kannapolis) & 41 Cabarrus Ave W (Concord); **Food Lion** & **Family Dollar**, Oak Avenue Mall (Oak Ave & Vance St)
- **NEWSPAPER**
  Independent Tribune, www.independenttribune.com

RALEIGH (pop. 403,892), Wake County; Area Codes: 919, 984
Incorporated 1794, originally known as Wake Court House until selected as state's capital in 1792 and named for Sir Walter Raleigh
Amtrak Station (RGH): 320 W. Cabarrus St; Tel: 919-833-7594
Buses: CAT, Triangle Transit, Greyhound & Wolfline (NC State University)
CAT Route Map:
www.raleighnc.gov/services/content/PWksTransit/Articles/CATBusRoutes.html
City website: www.raleighnc.gov

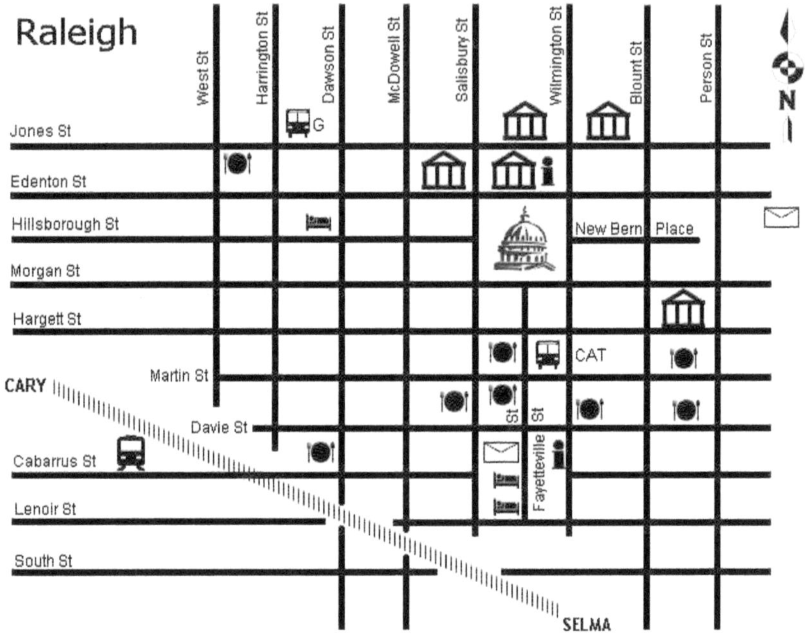

- **ATTRACTIONS** (downtown unless noted)
  NC Museum of History, 5 E. Edenton St; **NC Museum of Natural Sciences**, 11 W. Jones St; **NC Sports Hall of Fame**, 5 E. Edenton St; **Raleigh City Museum**, 220 Fayetteville St; **Marbles Kids Museum**, 201 E. Hargett St; **NC Executive Mansion**, 200 N. Blount St; **Haywood Hall House and Gardens**, 211 New Bern Pl; **Historic Oakwood**, 100-700 blocks of N. Person St; **Joel Lane Museum House**, 728 W. Hargett St; **Mordecai Historic Park**, 1 Mimosa St; **NC State Archives**, 109 E. Jones St; **North Carolina State Capitol**, Union Square (1 E. Edenton St); **NC State Legislative Building**, 16 W. Jones St; **Saint Augustine's College Historic Chapel**, 1315 Oakwood Ave; **NC Museum of Art**, 2110 Blue Ridge Rd (out of downtown);
- **FOOD** (downtown)
  Subway, 126 S. Salisbury/220 E. Martin St; **Poole's Diner**, 426 S. McDowell St (dinner only, Tue-Sun); **Beasley's Chicken & Honey** and **Chuck's**, 237 S. Wilmington St; **Big Ed's**, 220 Wolfe St; **Cooper's Barbeque**, 109 E. Davie St; **The Plaza Café**, 411 Fayetteville St; **42nd St Oyster Bar**, 508 W. Jones St; **Natty Greene's Pub**, 505 W. Jones St; **Krispy Kreme**, 549 N. Person St; New Oakwood Café, 300 E. Edenton St; **Angelo's**, 200 E. Martin St; **Gravy**, 135 S. Wilmington St; **Tir na nOg Irish Pub**, 218 S.

Blount St; **Boylan Bridge Brew Pub**, 210 S. Boylan Ave; more to be found at www.visitraleigh.com/visitors/restaurants/

- **LODGING** (downtown or *close by)
  Clarion Hotel State Capital, 320 Hillsborough St; **Days Inn Downtown Raleigh**, 300 N. Dawson St; **Oakwood Inn B&B**, 411 N. Bloodworth St; **Raleigh Marriott City Center**, 500 Fayetteville St; **Sheraton Raleigh Hotel**, 421 S. Salisbury St; **Holiday Inn Brownstone**, 1710 Hillsborough St*
- **OTHER** (downtown)
  Post Office, 300 Fayetteville St; **Public Library** (Cameron Village branch), **Courthouse**, 316 Fayetteville St; **Police**, 218 W. Cabarrus St;
- **NEWSPAPER**
  News & Observer, www.newsobserver.com

RALEIGH SKYLINE FROM TRAIN, author photo

ROCKY MOUNT (pop. 57,477), Nash and Edgecombe Counties; Area Code: 252
Incorporated 1867, named for rocky mounds and ledges on the site near the Tar River
Amtrak Station (RMT): 101 Coastline St; Tel: 252-446-3646
Buses: 111 Coastline St (Tar River Transit "TRT" & Greyhound)
TRT Route Maps: www.rockymountnc.gov/trt/routes.html
City website: www.rockymountnc.gov

- **ATTRACTIONS** (downtown unless noted)
  Rocky Mount Visitors Center (inside Amtrak Station, 2nd Floor); **Imperial Centre for the Arts and Sciences**, 270 Gay St (walk 0.7 mi. N), closed Monday; **Rocky Mount Fire Museum**, 404 S. Church St (8:30am-5:00pm, M-F); **Bel Air Artisans Center**, 115 S. Church St (walk 0.4 mi. N), 10-5 open daily except Sunday; **Booker T Theater**, 125 E. Thomas St (walk 0.6 mi. NE), interior by appointment; **North Carolina Wesleyan College**, 3400 N. Wesleyan Blvd (taxicab 6.0 mi.); **City Trail System** (distance varies; details at www.rockymountnc.gov/parks); **Rocky Mount Railroad Depot** (Amtrak Station; good location for watching freight and passenger trains); **Rocky Mount Veterans' Memorial** (Jack Laughery Park), 321 N. Church St;
- **FOOD** (downtown)
  Subway (1), 215 NE Main St (walk 0.5 mi. NE), Mon-Fri 7am-7pm, Sat-Sun 10am-3pm; **Central Café (2)** (diner), 132 S. Church St (walk 0.3 mi. N), B/L/D M-Sa, closed Sunday; **Taste of Paradise (3)** (Caribbean), 101 Atlantic Ave (walk 0.5 mi. NE) L/D TWThSa, B/L/D Fri, closed Sunday and Monday
- **LODGING** (out of downtown)
  Doubletree by Hilton, 651 N. Winstead Ave (taxicab 5.6 mi.); **Holiday Inn**, 200 Enterprise Dr (taxicab 5.9 mi. or TRT Rte. 7)
- **OTHER** (downtown)
  Post Office, 201 S. George St (0.5 mi. E, walk or TRT Rte. 2); **Public Library**, 727 N. Grace St (walk 0.8 mi. N, or TRT Rte. 5); **Courthouse**, 234 W. Washington St (Nashville); **Police**, One Government Plaza;

• **NEWSPAPER**

Rocky Mount Telegram, www.rockymounttelegram.com

ROCKY MOUNT VETERANS' MEMORIAL WITH IMPERIAL CENTRE IN BACKGROUND, author photo

ROWAN MUSEUM, SALISBURY, author photo

SALISBURY (pop. 33,662), Rowan County; Area Code: 704
Incorporated 1755, named either for the city in England or the one in Maryland
Amtrak Station (SAL): 215 Depot St; Tel: 704-639-7728
Buses: STS (Salisbury Transit System) & Greyhound
STS Route Maps: www.salisburync.gov/transit/route2011.pdf
City website: www.salisburync.gov

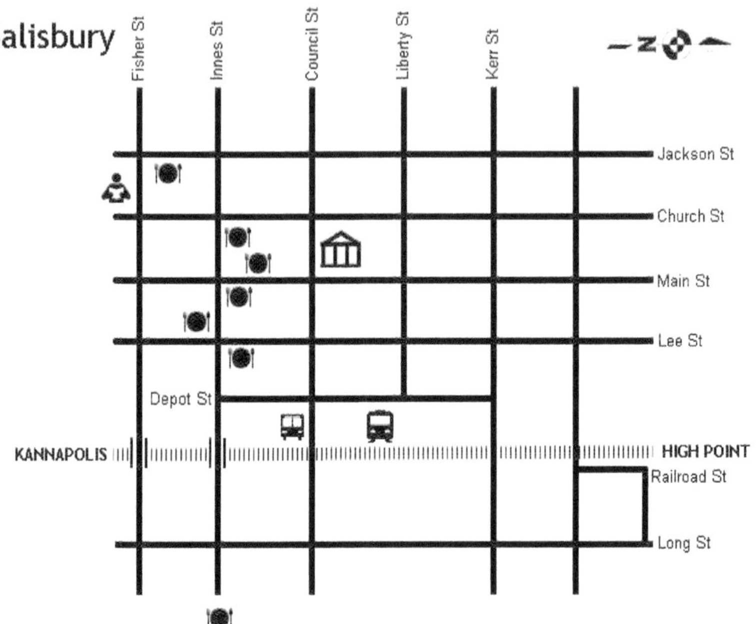

- **ATTRACTIONS** (downtown unless noted)
  Salisbury Depot, at Amtrak Station; **NC Transportation Museum**, 400 S. Salisbury St (Spencer); **Clydes** (museum, 224 E. Bank St); **Old County Courthouse**, 202 N. Main St; **Heritage Tour**, http://www.ci.salisbury.nc.us/heritage_tour.html
- **FOOD** (downtown)
  Subway, 910 W. Innes St; **La Cava**, 329 S. Church St; **Cartucci's**, 105 E. Fisher St; **Salty Caper**, 115 S. Lee St; **Uncle Buck's All-American Pub**, 117 E. Innes St; **Chef Santos**, 123 E. Fisher St; **Wong's**, 108 E. Council St**; Spanky's Ice-Cream & Sandwiches**, 101 N. Main St; **Hap's Grill**, 116 ½ N. Main St; **Sweet Meadow Café**, 118 W. Innes St; **Richard's Bar-B-Q**, 522 N. Main St; **Wrenn House**, 115 S. Jackson St; also see, www.visitsalisburync.com/restaurants/
- **LODGING**
  Lodging Guide, www.visitsalisburync.com/lodging/
- **OTHER** (downtown)
  Post Office, 605 E. Innes St; **Public Library**, 201 W. Fisher St; **Courthouse**, 210 N. Main St; **Police**, 130 E. Liberty St (Salisbury) & 600 S. Salisbury Ave (Spencer);
- **NEWSPAPER**
  Salisbury Post, www.salisburypost.com

SELMA (pop. 6,073), Johnston County; Area Code: 919
Incorporated 1873, originally known as Mitchenor's Station after local business
Amtrak Station (SSM): 500 E. Railroad St; Tel: 919-965-6971
Buses: Greyhound (Smithfield)
City website: www.selma-nc.com

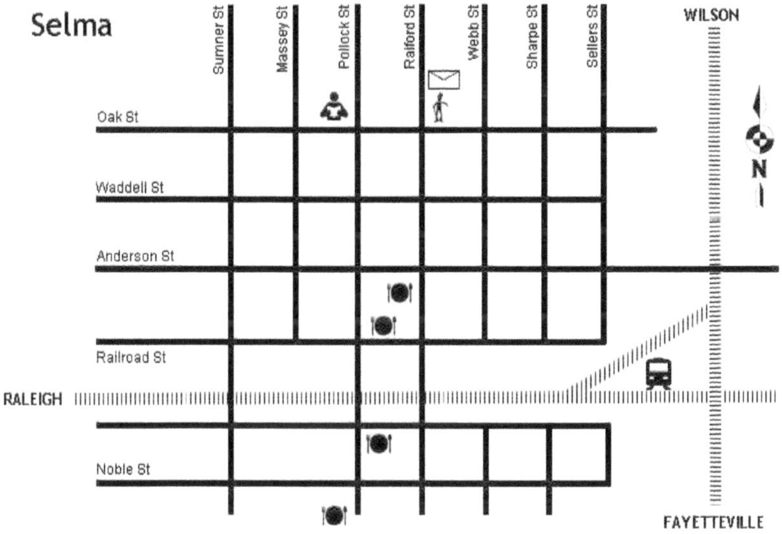

- **ATTRACTIONS** (downtown unless noted)
  Ava Gardner Museum, 325 E. Market St (Smithfield);
- **FOOD** (downtown)
  Hula Girl Sandwich Shop, 106 W. Railroad St; **Alondra's**, 308 S. Pollock St; **Pizza Xpress**, 201 S. Pollock St; **Sweetwater's Grille & Cheesecake Company**, 112 S. Raiford St; also see www.visitselma.org/places-to-eat
- **LODGING**
  Three Sisters B&B, 211 N. Raiford St; also see www.visitselma.org/places-to-stay
- **OTHER** (downtown)
  Post Office, 308 N. Raiford St; **Public Library**, 301 N. Pollock St (Selma) & 305 E. Market St (Smithfield); **Courthouse**, 207 E. Johnston St (Smithfield); **Police**, 201 N. Webb St (Selma) & 110 S. Fifth St (Smithfield);
- **NEWSPAPER**
  Smithfield Herald, www.smithfieldherald.com

SOUTHERN PINES (pop. 12,334); Moore County; Area Code: 910
Incorporated 1887, known earlier as "Vineland" but unacceptable (duplication) to US Post Office, therefore changed to reflect its location on edge of long leaf pine belt
Amtrak Station (SOP): 235 NW Broad St; Tel: 800-872-7245 (800-USA-RAIL)
Buses: none
Town website: www.southern pines.net

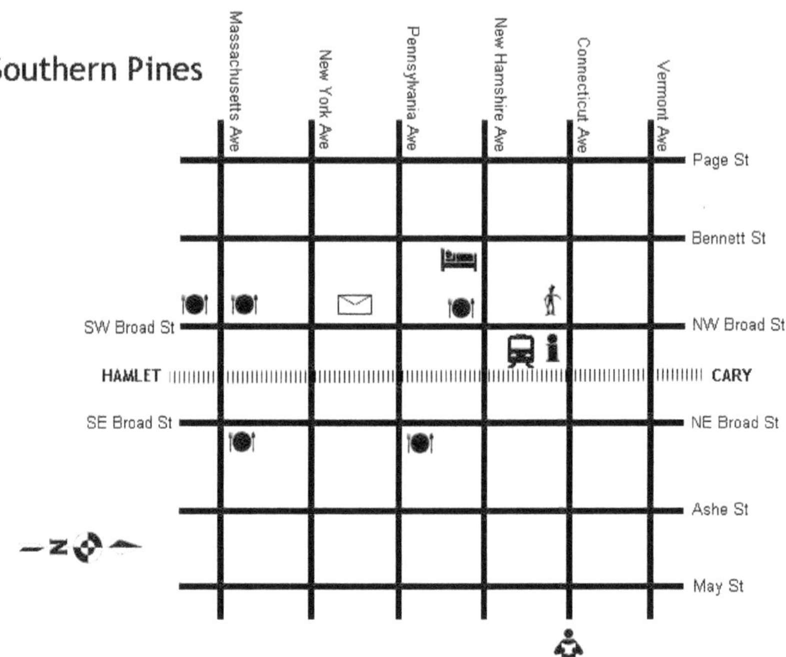

- **ATTRACTIONS** (downtown, unless noted)
  Southern Pines Historic District, Broad St; **NC Taxidermy Hall of Fame** (in Christian Book Store), 156 NW Broad St; **Sunrise Theater**, 250 NW Broad St; also see www.homeofgolf.com/map/
- **FOOD** (downtown)
  Lula's Café, 290 SW Broad St; **Sweet Basil**, 134 NW Broad St; **Mac's Breakfast Anytime**, 311 SE Broad St; **Flynne's Coffee Bar**, 115 NE Broad St; **Java Bean Plantation**, 410 SW Broad St; **Swank**, 124 W. Pennsylvania Ave; also see www.homeofgolf.com/map/
- **LODGING** (downtown, unless noted)
  Jefferson Inn, 150 W. New Hampshire Ave (near Amtrak Station); **Knollwood House B&B**, 1495 W. Connecticut Ave; **Midland Rd Manor B&B**, 1625 Midland Rd; also see www.homeofgolf.com/map/
- **OTHER** (downtown)
  Post Office, 190 SW Broad St; **Public Library**, 482 E. Connecticut Ave; **Police**, 801 SE Service Rd;
- **NEWSPAPER**
  Pilot, www.thepilot.com

WILSON (pop. 49,167); Wilson County; Area Code: 252
Incorporated 1849, earlier called "Toisnot Depot", named after Captain Louis D. Wilson who died at Vera Cruz in 1847 during War with Mexico
Amtrak Station (WLN): 401 E. Nash St; Tel: 252-246-1060
Buses: Wilson Transit System (WTS) & Greyhound
WTS Route Maps:
WTS System Map: http://www.wilsonnc.org/attachments/pages/217/busmap.pdf
City website: www.wilsonnc.org

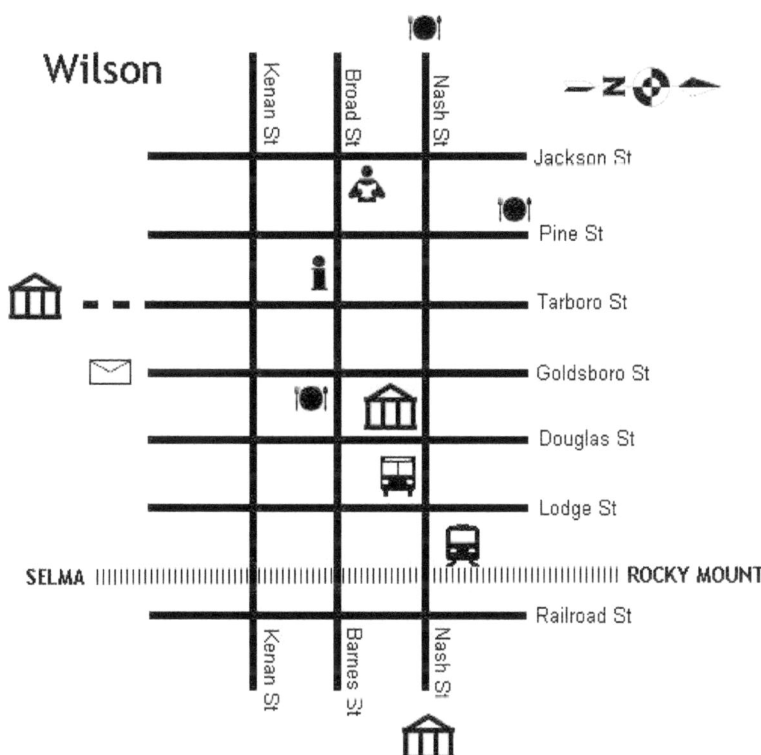

- **ATTRACTIONS** (downtown unless noted)
  Imagination Station Science Museum, 224 E. Nash St; **Freeman Round House** (not a railroad roundhouse, a true round house), 1202 Nash St SE (WTS Red Rte Woodard & Finch); **Wilson Visitors Center**, 209 Broad St; **NC Baseball Museum**, 300 Stadium St (WTS Blue Rte Regency Plaza)
- **WALKING TOUR**
  See www.wilson-nc.com/50things.cfm
- **FOOD** (downtown, unless noted)
  Worrell's Seafood Restaurant, 213 S. Goldsboro St; **Dick's Hot Dog Stand**, 1500 W. Nash St; **Sweet Maria's Bistro & Café**, 411 W. Nash St; **Jarman House**, 204 E. Green St; , also see www.wilson-nc.com/DiningResults.cfm
- **LODGING** (out of downtown)
  Lodging Guide, www.wilson-nc.com/lodging.cfm

- **OTHER** (downtown)
  Post Office, 501 Mercer St, SW; **Public Library**, 249 Nash St W; **Courthouse**, 115 Nash St E; **Police**, 120 N. Goldsboro St;
- **NEWSPAPER**
  Wilson Daily Times, www.wilsontimes.com

IMAGINATION STATION SCIENCE MUSEUM IN WILSON, author photo

WINSTON-SALEM (pop. 229,617), Forsyth County; Area Code:
Formed in 1913 by consolidation of Winston (inc. 1949) and Salem (inc 1856)
Amtrak Station: High Point (**HPT**, via NC Amtrak Connector)
Buses: WSTA, PART, Greyhound (Fifth St between Trade & Liberty Sts)
WSTA Route Map: www.wstransit.com/routes/Day-Routes.pdf
City website: www.cityofws.org

- **ATTRACTIONS** (downtown unless noted)
  Old Salem, 600 S. Main St (www.oldsalem.org); **Museum of Early Southern Decorative Arts**, 924 S. Main St; **Visitor Center**, 200 Brookstown Ave; also see www.visitwinstonsalem.com
- **FOOD** (downtown)
  Subway, 8 W. 3rd St/616 W. 4th St; **6th & Vine Wine Bar & Café**, 209 W. 6th St; **Bernardin's Restaurant**, 901 W. 4th St; Bib's, 675 W. 5th St; **Brew Nerds**, 305 W. 4th St; **Caffe Prada**, 390 N. Broad St; **Camino Bakery**, 310 W. 4th St; also see http://visitwinstonsalem.com/directory/dining
- **LODGING** (downtown)
  Embassy Suites, 460 N. Cherry St; **Marriott**, 425 N. Cherry; **Historic Brookstown Inn**,

200 Brookstown Ave; **Royal Inn**, 200 S. Broad St; Hawthorne Inn, 420 High St; also see www.visitwinstonsalem.com/directory/accommodations

- **OTHER** (downtown)
  Post Office, 1500 N. Patterson Ave (not downtown); **Public Library**, 660 W. 5th St; **Courthouse**, 200 N. Main St; **Police**, 725 N. Cherry St;
- **NEWSPAPER**
  Winston-Salem Journal, www.journalnow.com

STREET VIEW IN OLD SALEM, author photo

Part 4

THEME TRIPS

If this book has not already convinced you to plan and take a train trip, here is some additional information that might just seal the deal. If you like antiques, or art galleries, breweries, churches, civil war monuments, festivals, gardens, monuments and statues, sports, theaters, there is plenty to keep you busy. Also, a list of convenient urgent care clinics and hospitals is provided, just in case. Please note that the information is believed correct as of publication date; please check the correctness before you make your trip; some businesses may have closed.

ANTIQUES (downtown unless noted)

Burlington

- Old Timey Place Antiques, 342 S. Worth St; Granddaddy's Antiques, 2316 Maple Ave (not downtown)

Cary

- Streets of London Antiques (furniture), 928 W. Chatham St; Fairgrounds Flea Market (Sa/Su), Hillsborough St & Blue Ridge Rd, Raleigh (no bus service);

Charlotte

- South End Exchange (furniture), 1616 Camden Rd (LYNX Bland, walk); Sleepy Poet Antique Mall, 4450 South Blvd (LYNX Woodlawn, walk); North Davidson Arts District (NoDa), www.noda.org (mainly arts, CATS Rte 3 The Plaza)

Fayetteville

- The Cotton Exchange, 224 Donaldson St; The Shops at 214 Hay Street, 214 Hay St

Gastonia

- Katy Did Antiques & Gifts, 140 E. Main Ave

Greensboro

- Rhyne's Corner Cupboard Antiques, 603 S. Elm St; Mary's Antiques, 607 S. Elm St; Antiques & Accessories on Elm, 323 S. Elm St; The Farmer's Wife Antiques & Flowers, 339 S. Davie St; Lion's Crown Antiques, 104 Barnhardt St

High Point

- Lion House Antiques, 211 E. Commerce Ave; Antiques & Interiors, 317 N. Main St; Calico Collection, 711 N. Main St

Kannapolis

- Antique Mall at Cannon Village, 104 S. Main St; The Depot at Gibson Mill, 325 McGill Ave (Concord); Antique Market of Concord, 37 Union St S (Concord); Olde Concord Antiques, 14 Union St S (Concord); Another Time Around, 85 Buffalo Ave NW (Concord); Southern Comfort, 632 Church St N (Concord); Concord Clock Shop & Antiques, 247 Branchview Dr SE (Concord)

Raleigh

- Father & Son Antiques, 107 W. Hargett St; Antiques Emporium, 2060 Clark Ave (Cameron Village, CAT Rte 16 Oberlin Rd); Fairgrounds Flea Market (Sa/Su), Hillsborough St & Blue Ridge Rd, Raleigh (no bus service)

Rocky Mount

- Carriage House Curiosity Shop, 116 SW Main St; Shehadeh Antiques, 401 S. Washington St

Salisbury

- Salisbury Emporium, 230 E. Kerr St; Salisbury Square Antiques, 111 S. Main St; A Step in Time, 500 W.. Council St; Antiquarius, 118 N. Main St; Caniche, 200 S. Main St; Eighteen-Thirty-Nine Antiques, 218 W. Cemetery St

Selma

- throughout downtown area, www.antiquesselma.com (RECOMMENDED)

Southern Pines

- Theatre Antiques, 143 NE Broad St; Rose Cottage Antiques, 290 W. Pennsylvania Ave; Pond Hill House, 122 W. Pennsylvania Ave; Page Furniture, 130 E. Illinois Ave

Winston-Salem

- Brookstown Antiques, 1004 Brookstown Ave; NC Art & Antiques, 1590 Peters Creek Pkwy (WSTA Rte 23 Forsyth Tech, Peters Ck & Link Rd stop)

ART GALLERIES

Burlington

- Alamance Artisans Guild, 320 E. Davis St; Burlington Artists League, 170 Huffman Mill Rd (not downtown)

Cary

- Cary Gallery of Artists/Emerge Fine Art/Chambers Art, 200 S. Academy St

Charlotte

- North Davidson Arts District (NoDa), www.noda.org; Elder Gallery, 1427 South Blvd; The Light Factory, 345 N. College St; McColl Fine Art, 126 Cottage Pl; Providence Gallery, 601A Providence Rd; Pura Vida Worldly Art, 3202A N. Davidson St; Renee George Gallery, 225 E. Worthington Ave

Durham

- Durham Art Guild, 120 Morris St; LabourLove Gallery, 807 E. Main St; Nasher Museum of Art, 2001 Campus Dr (Duke University)

Fayetteville

- The Arts Council, 301 Hay St; Cape Fear Studios, 148 Maxwell St; Gallery ONE13, 113 Gillespie St; Old Town Gallery, 124 Maxwell St; City Center Gallery & Books, 112 Hay St

Gastonia

- Gaston County Art Guild, 212 W. Main Ave; The Art Station, 170 S. South St

Greensboro

- Ambleside Gallery (& Tea Room), 528 S. Elm St; The Artery Gallery, 1711 Spring Garden Rd; Tyler White Gallery, 307 State St;

High Point

- Theatre Art Galleries, 220 E. Commerce Ave; Lauren Galleries, 211 E. Commerce

Kannapolis

- Cabarrus Arts Council, 65 Union St S (Concord); Adam Ramsey Miller Gallery, 21 Union St S (Concord)

Raleigh

- Artspace, 201 E. Davie St; Moore Square Art District, Blount & Martin Sts; Municipal Building Art Exhibitions, 222 W. Hargett St; Pullen Arts Center, 105 Pullen Rd; Visual Arts Exchange, 325 Blake St

Rocky Mount

- Imperial Center for the Arts & Sciences, 270 Gay St; Bel Air Artisans Center, 115 S. Church St

Salisbury

- Waterworks Visual Art Center, 123 E. Liberty St; RailWalk Gallery, 409 N. Lee St; Fine Frame Gallery, 105 S. Main St; Southern Spirit Gallery, 102 S. Main St; Pottery 101, 101 S. Main St; Duck Blind Gallery, 107 S. Main St; Cascade Sculpture, 405 N. Lee St; Green Goat Gallery, 516 S. Salisbury Ave (Spencer); complete listing at: http://www.visitsalisburync.com/things-to-do/artworks-galleries/default.aspx

Selma

- Jen Owens Art Gallery, 101 N. Raiford St

Southern Pines

- Eye Candy Gallery and Wine Bar, 275 NE Broad St; Artist Alley, 167 E. New Hampshire Ave; Arts Council of Moore County, 482 E. Connecticut Ave (M-F, 9-5)

Wilson

- Arts Council of Wilson, 124 Nash St SW; Barton (College) Art Galleries, Whitehead & Gold Sts (WTS Orange Rte); Studio One of Wilson, 407 Nash St W; Imagination Station Art Gallery, 224 E. Nash St;

Winston-Salem

- Artworks Gallery, 564 N. Trade St; Downtown Arts District (www.dadaws.org); Piedmont Craftsmen Gallery, 601 N. Trade St

BREWERIES (in or close to downtown)

Charlotte

- NoDa Brewing Company, 2229 N. Davidson St
- Rock Bottom Restaurant & Brewery, 401 N. Tryon St
- The Olde Mecklenburg Brewery, 215 Southside Dr
- Triple C Brewing Company, 2900 Griffith St

Durham

- Bull City Burger & Brewery, 107 E. Parrish St
- Fullsteam. 726 E. Rigsbee Ave
- Triangle Brewing Company, 918 Pearl St

Fayetteville

- Huske Hardware House Restaurant & Brewery, 405 Hay St
- Mash House Brewery & Chop House, 4150 Sycamore Dairy Rd (not downtown)

Greensboro

- Natty Greene's Pub & Brewing Company, 345 S. Elm St
- Red Oak Brewery, 6901 Konica Dr (Whitsett)

High Point
- Liberty Steakhouse & Brewery, 914 Mall Loop Rd (not downtown)

Raleigh
- Natty Greene's Pub & Brewing Company, 504 W. Jones St
- Boylan Bridge Brewpub, 201 S. Boylan Ave
- Big Boss Brewing Company, 1249 Wicker Dr (not downtown)
- LoneRider Brewing Company, 8816 Gulf Ct (not downtown)
- Roth Brewing Company, 5907 Triangle Dr (not downtown)

Winston-Salem
- Foothills Brewing, 638 W 4th St

CHURCHES (historic, downtown unless noted)

Burlington
- First Presbyterian Church of Burlington, 508 W. Davis St
- Episcopal Church of the Holy Comforter, 320 E. Davis St
- First Baptist Church, 400 S. Broad St
- Davis Street United Methodist Church, 606 E. Davis St

Cary
- First United Methodist Church, 117 S. Academy St
- First Baptist Church, 218 S. Academy St

Charlotte
- First Presbyterian, 200 W. Trade St
- First United Methodist Church, 501 N. Tryon St
- St. Peter's Catholic Church, 507 S. Tryon St
- St. Peter's Episcopal Church, 115 W. Seventh St

Durham
- Duke Memorial United Methodist Church, 504 W. Chapel Hill St
- Duke Chapel,100 Chapel Dr, Duke University West Campus, www.chapel.duke.edu
- Ephphatha Church, 220 W. Geer St (free)

Fayetteville
- First Presbyterian Church, 102 Ann St
- Hay Street United Methodist Church, 320 Hay St
- First Baptist Church, 201 Anderson St
- St. John's Episcopal Church, 302 Green St
- St. Joseph's Episcopal Church, 509 Ramsey St

Gastonia
- First United Methodist Church, 190 E. Franklin Blvd
- St. Michael's Catholic Church, 708 St. Michael's Lane
- St. Mark's Episcopal Church, 258 W. Franklin Blvd
- St. Stephen's AME Zion Church, 201 W. Franklin St
- Loray Baptist Church, 1001 W. 2nd St

Greensboro
- First Presbyterian Church, 617 N. Elm St
- Holy Trinity Episcopal Church, 607 N. Greene St
- West Market Street United Methodist Church, 302 W. Market St

- Grace United Methodist Church, 438 W. Friendly St

Hamlet

- First Baptist Church, 208 Charlotte St
- Second Baptist Church, 518 4th St
- All Saints Episcopal Church, 217 Henderson St
- First United Methodist Church, 300 Charlotte St
- First Presbyterian Church, 200 Rice St

High Point

- First Presbyterian Church, 918 N. Main St
- First Baptist Church, 401 N. Main St

Kannapolis

- Kimball Memorial Lutheran Church, 101 Vance St
- Trinity United Methodist Church, 416 E. 1st St
- Centerview Baptist Church, 415 Walter St
- Central United Methodist Church, 30 Union St N (Concord)
- St. James Lutheran Church, 104 Union St S (Concord)
- Grace Lutheran Church, 58 Chestnut Dr SW (Concord)
- Impact Church International, 44 Cabarrus Ave W (Concord)

Raleigh

- First Baptist Church, 99 N. Salisbury St
- Christ Church, 120 E. Edenton St
- Unity Church of the Triangle, 118 S. Person St
- Church of the Good Shepherd, 125 Hillsborough St
- St Paul AME Zion Church, 402 W. Edenton St
- Sacred Heart Cathedral, 200 Hillsborough St

Rocky Mount

- Church of the Good Shepherd, 231 N. Church St
- First United Methodist Church, 100 S. Church St
- First Baptist Church, 200 S. Church St
- St. John AME Zion Church, 250 Atlantic Ave
- Our Lady of Perpetual Help, 315 Hammond St

Salisbury

- Sacred Heart Catholic Church, 375 Lumen Christie Lane
- St. John's Lutheran Church, 200 W. Innes St
- First United Methodist Church, 217 S. Church St
- First Presbyterian Church, 308 W. Fisher St
- St. Luke's Episcopal Church, 131 W. Council St
- First United Church of Christ, 207 W. Horah St

Selma

- Mt. Livingstone United Holy Church, 403 S. Ethel St
- St John AME Zion Church, 400 W. Watson St
- Edgerton Memorial United Methodist Church, 401 W. Anderson St
- First Missionary Baptist Church, 500 S. Pollock St

Southern Pines

- St. Anthony of Padua Catholic Church, 175 E. Connecticut Ave
- First Baptist Church, 200 E. New York Ave

- Brownson Memorial Presbyterian Church, 330 S. May St
- Church of God, 580 W. New Hampshire Ave
- Emmanuel Episcopal Church, 350 E. Massachusetts Ave

Wilson

- First Baptist Church, 311 Nash St W
- First United Methodist Church, 100 Green St NE
- St. Timothy's Episcopal Church, 202 Goldsboro St E
- Grace Baptist Church, 202 Kincaid Ave N

Winston-Salem

- First Presbyterian Church, 300 Cherry St N
- Centenary United Methodist Church, 646 W. 5th St
- Home Moravian Church, 529 S. Church St
- First Baptist Church, 501 W. 5th St
- St. Paul's Episcopal Church, 520 Summit St

FESTIVALS and SHOWS

Burlington

- Carousel Festival (September) www.burlingtonnc.gov/index.aspx?NID=867

Cary

- Lazy Daze Arts & Crafts Festival (August) www.townofcary.org/Page593.aspx
- Apex PeakFest (May) www.apexpeakfest.com

Charlotte

- Ulysses Spring Festival of the Arts (March) www.facebook.com/UlyssesCLT
- Festival in the Park (September) www.festivalinthepark.org/
- BBQ and Blues (October) www.charlottebbqandblues.com
- Food Lion Speed Street Festival (May) www.600festival.com

Durham

- The Taste of Durham (October) www.tasteofdurham.org
- American Dance Festival (June/July) www.americandance festival.org
- Bull Durham Blues Festival (Sept, 1st week)
- Full Frame Documentary Film Festival (April) www.fullframefest.org

Fayetteville

- Dogwood Festival (April, 4th weekend) www.faydogwoodfestival.com

Gastonia

- Catawba Indian Festival (June)
- Piedmont Heritage Festival (November)

Greensboro

- Festival Italiano (October)
- Eastern Music Festival (June, July) www.easternmusicfestival.org/
- Christmas Crafts Show (November)

Hamlet

- Seaboard Festival (October, last Saturday) www.hamletnc.us/seaboard.htm

High Point

- Furniture Market (April & October) www.highpointmarket.org
- John Coltrane Int'l Jazz & Blues Festival (September) coltranejazzfest.com

Kannapolis
- Spring Herb & Plant Festival (Concord, April) www.piedmont-farmersmarket.com
- Village Fest Arts & Crafts (May) www.cabarrusevents.org/id58.html

Lexington (special train stop)
- Lexington Barbecue Festival (October) www.barbecuefestival.com

Raleigh
- State Fair (October 3rd week) www.ncstatefair.org
- International Festival of Raleigh (September) www.internationalfestival.org
- Artsplosure (May 19-20, 2012) www.artsplosure.org
- Hopscotch Music Festival (September) www.hopscotchmusicfest.com

Rocky Mount
- Eastern NC BBQ Throw Down (October) www.bbqthrowdown.net

Salisbury
- Autumn Jubilee (October) www.dannicholas.net/ads_jubilee.aspx
- NC Transportation Museum, Spencer (special events) www.nctrans.org

Selma
- Railroad Days (October, 1st weekend) www.selma-nc.com
- Ham & Yam Festival (May, Smithfield) www.downtownsmithfield.com

Southern Pines
- Springfest (April, last Saturday) www.southernpines.biz/events/springfest/
- Palustris Festival (March) www.palustrisfestival.com

Wilson
- Whirligig Festival (November, 1st weekend) www.wilsonwhirligigfestival.com

Winston-Salem
- Festival of Books (September) www.bookmarksfestival.org
- Magnolia Baroque Festival (May)

GARDENS (public, downtown unless noted)

Burlington
- City of Burlington Parks, www.ci.burlington.nc.us/index.aspx?NID=233

Cary
- Cary Town Parks, www.townofcary.org

Charlotte
- McGill Rose Garden, 940 N. Davidson; Wing Haven Garden & Bird Sanctuary, 248 Ridgewood Ave; Botanical Gardens (UNC Charlotte), 9201 University City Blvd

Durham
- Magic Wings Butterfly House (NC Museum of Life & Science), 433 W. Murray Ave; Sarah P. Duke Gardens (Duke University), 420 Anderson St;

Fayetteville
- Cape Fear Botanical Garden, 536 N. Eastern Blvd;

Gastonia
- Daniel Stowe Botanical Gardens, 6500 S. New Hope Rd (Belmont);

Greensboro
- Tanger Family Bicentennial Garden & Bog Garden, bounded by N. Holden Rd, Cornwallis Dr & Hobbs Rd; Greensboro Arboretum, 401 Ashland Drive (Lindley Pk)

High Point
- High Point Museum & Historical Park, 1859 E. Lexington Ave;

Kannapolis
- Memorial Garden at First Presbyterian Church, 36 Spring St SW (Concord)

Raleigh
- Raleigh Rose Garden, 301 Pogue St (CAT Rte 4 Rex Hospital); Raulston Arboretum, 4415 Beryl Rd; Jaycee Daylily Garden, 2405 Wade Ave; Ellen Mordecai Garden (small antebellum garden featuring herbs), 1 Mimosa St; WRAL Azalea Gardens, 2619 Western Blvd (CAT Rte 11 Avent Ferry); Martin Luther King, Jr. Memorial Gardens, 1300 Martin Luther King Jr. Blvd (CAT Rte 5 Biltmore Hills);

Rocky Mount
- Rocky Mount Veterans Memorial (Jack Laughery Park), 321 N. Church St

Salisbury
- Poet's and Dreamer's Garden (Livingstone College), 701 W. Monroe St; Catawba Ecological Preserve (Catawba College), 2300 W. Innes St

Southern Pines
- Weymouth Center for the Arts & Humanities, 555 E. Connecticut Ave;

Wilson
- Library Rose Garden, 249 W. Nash St; Wilson Rose Garden, 1800 Herring Ave (not downtown, WTS Blue Rte Jordan Homes); Wilson Botanical Gardens, 1806 Goldsboro St (not downtown, no bus service)

Winston-Salem
- Old Salem, 924 S. Main St; Reynolda Gardens (Wake Forest University), 2250 Reynolda Rd; Bethabara Park, 2417 Bethabara Rd;

MONUMENTS, STATUES, & CEMETERIES (in or close to downtown)

Burlington
- Alamance Memorial Park, 4035 S. Church St,
- St. Athanasius Protestant Episcopal Church, E. Webb & W. Broad, 1882
- Brown's Chapel, 1317 W. Davis St
- Pine Hill, bounded by S. Main St., S. Mebane St., E. Summit Ave. and E. Kitchin St

Cary
- Railroad Man (statue), Amtrak Station
- Hill Crest Cemetery, take S. Harrison Ave to Page St

Charlotte
- Elmwood Cemetery, 700 W. Sixth St
- Oaklawn Cemetery, 1615 Oaklawn Dr
- Pinewood Cemetery, 9th & Seaboard Sts
- Settlers Cemetery, 5th St between Church and Poplar
- Sugaw Creek Presbyterian Church Cemetery, 101 Sugar Creek Rd W
- Woodland United Presbyterian Church Cemetery, 900 Rhyne Rd

Durham
- Woodlawn Memorial Park, Holloway & Herbert Sts (DATA Rte 13)
- Maplewood Cemetery,Duke University Rd & Swift Ave (DATA Rte 6)
- Beechwood Cemetery, Cornwallis Rd at Jan Ct (DATA Rte 5)

Fayetteville
- Cross Creek Cemetery, Ann & Lamon Sts
- Cumberland Memorial Gardens, 4509 Raeford Rd
- Lafayette Memorial Park, 2301 Ramsey St

Gastonia
- Gastonia City Cemetery, 540 N. Broad St
- Gaston Memorial (Oakwood) Cemetery, S. Chester at W. Franklin St

Greensboro
- Public Art, http://downtowngreensboro.net/explore/attractions/public-art
- Forest Lawn (includes a veterans memorial), 3901 Forest Lawn Dr
- Green Hill, between Battleground Ave & Wharton St & Hill St
- Maplewood (includes a veterans memorial), Bingham St off E. Market St
- Union Cemetery, E. Whittington St & S. Elm St

Hamlet
- Mary Love Cemetery, Oakland Ave at Aberdeen St

High Point
- Plank Road Foreman (statue), Amtrak Station
- John Coltrane (statue), Commerce Ave & Hamilton St
- Veterans' Memorial Park (statue), corner of High St & Main St
- Oakwood Municipal Cemetery, 512 Steele St
- Floral Garden Memorial Park, 1730 W. English Rd

Kannapolis
- Dale Earnhardt Tribute Plaza, Main St between A & B Sts (statue and gardens)
- Kannapolis Cemetery, 700 W. C St

Raleigh
- Oakwood Cemetery, 701 Oakwood Ave,
- National Cemetery, 501 Rocky Quarry Rd,
- City Cemetery, 209 N. Dawson St
- Mount Hope Cemetery, 120 Prospect Ave, established by black citizens shortly after the Civil War in 1872
- O'Rourke ("Catholic") Cemetery, 1101 Pender St, established on land donated to the Catholic Church in 1858; was used as a potter's field; city-owned
- State Capitol www.nchistoricsites.org/capitol/

Rocky Mount
- Veterans Memorial, 321 N. Church St
- Rocky Mount City Cemetery, 436 Pineview St

Salisbury
- National Cemetery, 202 Government Rd; Confederate Monument, 200 W. Innes St;

Selma
- Selma City Cemetery, 100 S. Raiford Rd
- Selma Memorial Gardens, S. Pollock St at US 70 (not downtown)

Southern Pines
- Pinelawn Memorial Park, 1105 W. Morganton Rd
- Southern Pines Memorial Park, 482 E. Connecticut Ave

Wilson
- Peaceful Maplewood Cemetery and several historic churches are located in Old

Wilson; the (former) Primitive Baptist Church, First Christian Church, St. Timothy's Episcopal Church, and Our Redeemer Lutheran Church

Winston-Salem

- Salem Cemetery, Church St S;
- Winston-Salem City Cemetery, 2124 New Walkertown Rd (not downtown)

PARKS

Burlington

- City Park (1910 Dentzel Carousel), www.burlingtonnc.gov/index.aspx?NID=233
- City Parks, http://www.burlingtonnc.gov/index.aspx?NID=221

Cary

- Town Parks, www.townofcary.org/Departments/

Charlotte

- City/County Parks, http://charmeck.org/mecklenburg/county/ParkandRec/Parks/

Durham

- City Parks, www.durhamnc.gov/gis_apps/sp/parkapp/mainmap.cfm

Fayetteville

- NC Veterans Park, 300 Bragg Blvd, www.ncveteranspark.org
- City/County Parks, www.fcpr.us/parks.aspx

Gastonia

- City Parks, http://www.cityofgastonia.com/city_serv/parks/map/parkmap.cfm

Greensboro

- City Parks, www.greensboro-nc.gov/index.aspx?page=1151

Hamlet

- Hamlet Seaboard Station, http://www.hamletnc.us/station.htm

High Point

- City Parks, http://www.highpointnc.gov/pr/

Kannapolis

- Village Park, 710 W. C St (incl. Rotary Express Train, CP Huntington scale model)
- Dale Earnhardt Tribute Plaza, Main St between A & B Sts (statue and gardens)
- Veterans Park, N. Main and 1st St

Raleigh

- Pullen Park (Dentzel Carousel), www.raleighnc.gov/arts/content/PRecParks
- Moore Square, www.nps.gov/nr/travel/raleigh/moo.htm
- Union Square (State Capitol)
- City Parks, www.raleighnc.gov/arts/content/PRecParks/

Rocky Mount

- City Parks, www.rockymountnc.gov/parks/parks.html
- Tar River Walking & Biking Trail, www.rockymountnc.gov/parks/trails.html

Salisbury

- Dan Nicholas Park (Haden's Carousel) www.dannicholas.net/carousel.aspx
- City Parks, www.salisburync.gov/pkrec/Parks_Facilities/Parks.htm

Selma

- Town Parks, www.selma-nc.com

Southern Pines

- Town Parks, http://www.southernpines.net/recreation/parks.aspx

Wilson
- City Parks, www.wilsonnc.org/departments/parksandrecreation/facilities/

Winston-Salem
- City Parks, www.cityofws.org/Home/Departments/RecreationAndParks/

SPORTS

Burlington
- Burlington Royals (baseball) www.milb.com/index.jsp?sid=t483

Cary
- Carolina RailHawks (soccer) www.carolinarailhawks.com

Charlotte
- Carolina Panthers (NFL football) www.panthers.com
- Charlotte Bobcats (NBA basketball) www.nba.com/bobcats/
- Charlotte Knights (baseball) www.milb.com/index.jsp?sid=t494
- Charlotte Eagles (soccer) www.charlotteeagles.com
- Charlotte Checkers (AHL ice hockey) www.gocheckers.com

Durham
- Durham Bulls (baseball) www.milb.com/index.jsp?sid=t234

Fayetteville
- Fayetteville SwampDogs (baseball) www.goswampdogs.com
- Fayetteville FireAntz (ice hockey) www.fireantzhockey.com

Gastonia
- Gastonia Grizzlies (baseball) www.gastoniagrizzlies.com

Greensboro
- Greensboro Grasshoppers (baseball) www.milb.com/index.jsp?sid=t477
- Carolina Dynamo (soccer) www.carolinadynamo.com

Kannapolis
- Kannapolis Intimidators (baseball) www.milb.com/index.jsp?sid=t487

Raleigh
- Carolina Hurricanes (NHL ice hockey) hurricanes.nhl.com
- Carolina RailHawks (soccer) www.carolinarailhawks.com

Winston-Salem
- Winston-Salem Dash (baseball) www.milb.com/index.jsp?sid=t580

THEATERS; LIVE PERFORMANCES

Burlington
- Paramount, 128 E. Front St, ww.burlingtondowntown.com/paramount.htm

Cary
- Koka Booth Amphitheatre, 8003 Regency Pkwy, www.boothamphiteatre.com

Charlotte
- Blumenthal Performing Arts Center, 5th & College St, www.blumenthalarts.org
- Belk Theatre, 130 N. Tryon St, www.blumenthalarts.org
- Booth Playhouse, 130 N. Tryon St, www.blumenthalarts.org
- Duke Energy Theater at Spirit Square, 345 N. College St, www.blumenthalarts.org

- Knight Theater at Levine Center, 430 S. Tryon St, www.blumenthalarts.org
- McGlohon Theater at Spirit Square, 345 N. College St, www.blumenthalarts.org
- Stage Door Theater, 5th & College Sts, www.blumenthalarts.org
- Theatre Charlotte, 501 Queens Rd, www.theatrecharlotte.org
- Visulite Theatre, 1615 Elizabeth Ave, www.visulite.com
- The Music Factory, www.musicfactory.com
- Charlotte Symphony, www.charlottesymphony.org

Durham
- Durham Performing Arts Center (DPAC), 123 Vivian St, www.dpacnc.com
- Carolina Theater, 309 W. Morgan St, www.carolinatheatre.org
- Manbites Dog Theater, 703 Foster St, www.manbitesdogtheater.org
- Durham Symphony, www.durhamsymphony.org

Fayetteville
- Cape Fear Regional Theatre, 1209 Hay St, www.cfrt.org
- Gilbert Theater, 116 Green St, www.gilberttheater.com
- Fayetteville Symphony, www.fayettevillesymphony.org

Gastonia
- Little Theater of Gastonia, 238 S. Clay St, www.littletheaterofgastonia.com
- Gaston Chorale Society, www.gastonarts.org/gastonchoral.htm

Greensboro
- Carolina Theatre, 310 S. Greene St, www.carolinatheatre.com
- Community Theatre of Greensboro, 520 S. Elm St, www.ctgso.org
- Greensboro Ballet, 200 N. Davie St, www.greensboroballet.com
- Greensboro Symphony, www.greensborosymphony.org

High Point
- High Point Theatre, 220 E. Commerce Ave, www.highpointtheatre.com
- NC Shakespeare Festival, www.ncshakes.org

Kannapolis
- Gem, 111 W. 1st St, www.gem-theatre.com
- Davis, 65 Union St S (Concord), www.cabarrusartscouncil.org/davis-theatre/

Raleigh
- North Carolina Theatre, 1 E. South St, www.nctheatre.com
- Burning Coal Theatre, 224 Polk St, www.burningcoal.org
- NC Master Chorale, 227 W. Martin St, www.ncmasterchorale.org
- North Carolina Opera, 414 Fayetteville St, www.ncopera.org
- North Carolina Symphony, 2 E. South St, www.ncsymphony.org
- PineCone, 227 W. Martin St, www.pinecone.org
- Raleigh Chamber Music Guild, 227 W. Martin St, www.rcmg.org
- Raleigh Civic Symphony, 2620 Cates Ave, www.raleighcivicsymphony.org
- Raleigh Ensemble Players, 213 Fayetteville St, www.realtheatre.org
- Raleigh Little Theatre, 301 Pogue St, www.raleighlittletheatre.org
- Raleigh Symphony Orchestra, www.raleighsymphony.org
- Theatre In The Park, 107 Pullen Rd, www.theatreinthepark.com
- Meredith College, www.meredith.edu
- NC State University, www.ncsu.edu
- William Peace University, www.peace.edu

- St. Augustine's College, www.st-aug.edu
- Shaw University, www.shawuniversity.edu
- IMAX Theatre, 201 E. Hargett St, www.imaxraleigh.org

Rocky Mount
- Art Center Community Theatre, 270 Gay St, http://arts.imperialcentre.org
- Tar River Orchestra & Chorus, www.abouttroc.org/

Salisbury
- Piedmont Players Theatre, 135 E. Fisher St, www.piedmontplayers.com
- Salisbury Symphony Orchestra, www.salisburysymphony.org

Selma
- Rudy Theatre (American Music Jubilee), 300 N. Raiford St, www.amjubilee.com
- Neuse Little Theatre, 104 S. Front St (Smithfield), www.neuselittletheatre.org

Southern Pines
- Sunrise Theater, 250 NW Broad Street, www.sunrisetheater.com
- Carolina Philharmonic (Pinehurst), www.carolinaphil.org

Wilson
- Wilson Arts Center, 124 Nash St, www.wilsonarts.com
- Barton College/Wilson Symphony, www.barton.edu/culturalarts/symphony.asp

Winston-Salem
- Winston-Salem Symphony, www.wssymphony.org
- Winston-Salem Festival Ballet, www.winstonsalemfestivalballet.org/

URGENT CARE CLINICS & HOSPITALS

Information you hope you won't need.
For major medical emergencies, call 911

M (Monday), Tu (Tuesday), W (Wednesday), Th (Thursday), F (Friday), Sa (Saturday), Su (Sunday)

Burlington

NextCare Urgent Care, 1713 S Church St, 336-222-8888, M-F 8-7pm, Sa 8-2pm, Su 10-2pm
Hospital: Alamance Regional Medical Center, 1240 Huffman Mill Rd, 336-538-7000

Cary

Rex Urgent Care of Cary, 1515 SW Cary Pkwy, (919) 387-3180, M-F 9-5pm, Sa/Su closed
Hospitals: Rex Healthcare of Cary, 1505 & 1515 SW Cary Pkwy, 919-387-3140
WakeMed Cary, 1900 Kildaire Farm Rd, 919-350-2300

Charlotte

CVS Pharmacy MinuteClinic, 210 E. Trade St, M-F 8-7, Sa/Su Closed
Concentra Urgent Care, 1614 South Blvd, 704-338-1268, M-F 7:30-9pm, Sa/Su 10-6pm
Hospitals: Carolinas Medical Center, 1000 Blythe Blvd, 704-355-2000
Presbyterian Hospital, 200 Hawthorne Ln, 704-384-4000

Durham

Duke Urgent Care Center, 1901 Hillandale Rd, 919-383-4355, daily 8-8pm
Hospitals: Duke University Hospital, 2301 Erwin Rd, 888-275-3853
Durham Regional Hospital, 3643 Roxboro Rd, 919-470-4000
Veterans Administration Hospital, 508 Fulton St, 888-878-6890 (§)

Fayetteville

Cross Creek Urgent Care, 726 Ramsey St, 910-221-2200

MedEx Urgent Care, 504 Owen Dr, 910-221-3030
Haymount Urgent Care, 1909 Bragg Blvd, 910-484-1210, M-F 9-5pm, Sa/Su closed
NextCare Urgent Care, 217 Glensford Rd, 888-381-4858, M-Th 8-8pm, F-Su 8-12 midnight
Hospital: Cape Fear Valley Medical Center, 1638 Owen Dr, 910-615-4000
Veterans Administration Medical Center, 2300 Ramsey St, 800-771-6106 (§)

Gastonia

NextCare Urgent Care , 3680 Robinwood Rd, 888-381-4858, M-F 8-8pm, Sa/Su 8-4pm
Hospital: Gaston Memorial Hospital, 2525 Court Drive, 704-834-2000

Greensboro

CVS Pharmacy MinuteClinic, 605 College Rd, M-F 8:30-7:30pm, Sa 9-5:30pm, Su 10-5:30pm
Fast-Med Urgent Care/Greensboro, 3215 Battleground Ave, 336-387-5020, M-F 8-7:45pm, Sa 9-4:45pm, Su 10-5:45pm
OccuMed Walk-In & Urgent Care, 530 - C North Elam Ave, 336-574-0707, M-Tu 8-5pm, W-F 8-6pm, Sa by appointment, Su closed
Hospital: Moses H. Cone Memorial Hospital, 1200 N. Elm St, 336-832-7000

Hamlet

Hospitals: Sandhills Regional Medical Center, 1000 W. Hamlet Ave, 910-205-8000
Richmond Memorial Hospital, 925 Long Drive (Rockingham), 910-417-3000

High Point

Doctors Express, 1231 Eastchester Dr, 336-884-4050, M-F 8-8pm, Sa/Su 9-6pm
Hospital: High Point Regional Hospital, 601 N. Elm St, 336-878-6000

Kannapolis

Fast-Med Urgent Care (Concord), 391 GW Liles Pkwy NW, 704-886-1780, M-F 8:30-7:45pm, Sa 9-4:45pm, Su 10-4:45pm
Hospital: Carolinas Medical Center-NE, 920 Church St N (Concord), 704-403-3000

Raleigh

City Center Medical Group, Two Progress Plaza, 150 E. Davie Street, 919-834-5299, M-F 8-4:30pm, Sa/Su Closed
Hospitals: WakeMed, 3000 New Bern Ave, 919-350-8000
Duke Raleigh Hospital, 3400 Wake Forest Rd, 919-954-3000
Rex Hospital, 4420 Lake Boone Trail, 919-784-3100

Rocky Mount

Carolina Quick Care, 550 North Winstead Rd, 252-451-3411, 8-8pm daily
Hospital: Nash General Hospital, 2460 Curtis Ellis Dr, 252-443-8000

Salisbury

ProMed Minor Emergency Center, 628 W. Innes St, 704 637-8040, M-F 8-8pm, Sat 10-6pm, Sun 10-4pm
Hospital: Rowan Regional Medical Center, 612 Mocksville Ave, 704-210-5000
Veterans Administration Medical Center, 1601 Brenner Ave, 704-638-9000 (§)

Selma

QuikMed Urgent Care, 514 N Bright Leaf Blvd (Smithfield), M-F 9-5pm, Sa/Su closed
Hospital: Johnston Memorial Hospital, 509 N. Bright Leaf Blvd (Smithfield), 919-934-8171

Southern Pines

Hospital: Moore Regional Hospital, 155 Memorial Dr (Pinehurst), 910-715-1000

Wilson

Carolina Quick Care, 2503B Forest Hill Rd, 252-991-0555, 8-8pm daily
Hospital: Wilson Medical Center, 1705 Tarboro St SW, 252-399-8040

Winston-Salem

Fast-Med Urgent Care, 4937 Old Country Club Rd, 336-546-1666, M-F 8-7:45pm; Sat 9-4:45pm; Sun 10-5:45pm

CVS Pharmacy MinuteClinic, 3325 Robinhood Rd, M-F 8:30-7:30, Sat 9-5:30pm, Sun 10-5:30pm
Hospitals: Forsyth Medical Center, 3333 Silas Creek Pkwy, 336-718-5000
Wake Forest University Baptist Medical Center, Medical Center Blvd, 336-716-2011
(§) military service veterans only

COMMUNITIES SERVED BY GREYHOUND (G) or COACH AMERICA (CA)

Ahoskie: www.ahoskie.org (G)
Asheville: www.ashevillenc.gov University of NC at Asheville (G)
Blowing Rock: www.townofblowingrock.com (CA)
Boone: www.townofboone.net, Appalachian State University (CA)
Chapel Hill**: www.ci.chapel-hill.nc.us, University of North Carolina (*)
Edenton: www.townofedenton.com (G)
Elizabeth City: www.cityofec.com, Elizabeth City State University; US Coast Guard (G)
Goldsboro: www.ci.goldsboro.nc.us, Pope Air Force Base (G)
Greenville**: www.greenvillenc.gov, East Carolina University (G)
Henderson: www.ci.henderson.nc.us (G)
Hickory**: www.hickorync.gov (G) (CA)
Jacksonville: www.ci.jacksonville.nc.us, Camp Lejeune Marine Corps Base (G)
Kings Mountain: www.cityofkm.com
Kinston: www.ci.kinston.nc.us (G)
Laurinburg: www.laurinburg.org (G)
Lenoir: www.cityoflenoir.com (CA)
Lincolnton: www.ci.lincolnton.nc.us (CA)
Lumberton: www.ci.lumberton.nc.us (G)
Monroe: www.monroenc.org (CA)
New Bern: www.newbern-nc.org (G)
Rockingham: www.gorockingham.com (CA)
Smithfield: www.smithfield-nc.com (also see "Selma") (G)
Statesville: www.ci.statesville.nc.us (G)
Wadesboro: www.cityofwadesboro.org (CA)
Wallace: www.townofwallace.com (G)
Washington: www.washington-nc.com (G)
Williamston: www.townofwilliamston.com (G)
Wilmington**: www.wilmingtonnc.gov, University of NC at Wilmington (G)

* Triangle Transit: www.gotriangle.org/transit/maps-and-schedules/
** Local public transit available

ROCKY MOUNT AMTRAK STATION WITH RAILCAR DISPLAY, author photo

GREYHOUND BUS IN GREENSBORO, author photo

Appendix A

TRAVEL AND TOURISM WEBSITES

North Carolina	www.visitnc.com

NC Amtrak Communities

Burlington	www.visitalamance.com
Cary	www.visitraleigh.com
Charlotte	www.charlottesgotalot.com
Durham	www.durham-nc.com
Fayetteville	www.visitfayettevillenc.com
Gastonia	www.visitgaston.org
Greensboro	www.greensboronc.org
Hamlet	www.visitrichmondcounty.com
High Point	www.highpoint.org
Kannapolis/Concord	www.visitcabarrus.com
Raleigh	www.visitraleigh.com
Rocky Mount	www.rockymounttravel.com
Salisbury	www.visitsalisburync.com
Selma/Smithfield	www.visitselma.org
Southern Pines	www.homeofgolf.com
Wilson	www.wilson-nc.com
Winston-Salem	www.visitwinstonsalem.com

Other Communities

Ahoskie	www.ahoskiechamber.com
Asheville	www.exploreasheville.com
Boone/Blowing Rock	www.exploreboonearea.com
Edenton	www.visitedenton.com
Elizabeth City	www.discoverec.org
Goldsboro	www.greatergoldsboro.com
Greenville	www.visitgreenvillenc.com
Henderson	www.kerrlake-nc.com
Hickory	www.hickorymetro.com

Jacksonville	www.onslowcountytourism.com
Kings Mountain	www.tourclevelandcounty.com
Kinston	www.visitkinston.com
Laurinburg	www.laurinburgchamber.com
Lenoir	www.explorecladwell.com
Lincolnton	www.lincolnchambernc.org
Lumberton	www.lumberton-nc.com
Monroe	www.visitmonroenc.org
New Bern	www.visitnewbern.com
Rockingham	www.visitrichmondcounty.com
Statesville	www.visitstatesville.org
Wadesboro	www.uptownwadesboro.com
Wallace	www.wallacechamberofcommerce.com
Washington	www.washington-nc.com
Williamston	www.visitmartincounty.com

NCDOT RAIL DIVISION	www.bytrain.org
AMTRAK RESERVATIONS	www.amtrak.com

DURHAM AMTRAK STATION, author photo

Appendix B

BANKS IN CITIES WITH TRAIN STATIONS

Branches with ATM's, unless noted

Burlington

Wells Fargo, 500 S. Main St
Bank of America, 245 W. Davis St

Cary

BB&T, 200 E. Chatham St

Charlotte

Wells Fargo, 301 S. Tryon
Bank of America, 2 Bank of America Plaza
BB&T, 200 S. College St
SunTrust, 112 S. Tryon St
First Citizens, 128 S. Tryon St

Durham

PNC, 500 Morgan St
Wells Fargo, 201 N. Roxboro Rd (ATM only)
BB&T, 505 S. Duke St

Fayetteville

PNC, 454 Ramsey St
Wells Fargo, 200 Green St
Bank of America, 324 Mason St
BB&T, 300 Rowan St
First Citizens,130 Grove St; 100 Hay St (Airborne Museum., ATM only)

Gastonia

PNC, 100 E. Garrison Blvd
Wells Fargo, 110 E. Franklin Blvd
BB&T, 265 W. Franklin Blvd

Greensboro

PNC, 230 N. Elm St
Wells Fargo, 300 N. Greene St
Bank of America, 101 W. Friendly Ave
BB&T, 201 W. Market St
First Citizens, 100 S. Elm St

Hamlet

PNC, 114 Main St
BB&T, 8 Raleigh St

BANKS (continued)

High Point
Wells Fargo, 200 N. Main St
Bank of America, 501 N. Main St
BB&T, 620 N. Main St
First Citizens, 700 N. Main St

Kannapolis
Wells Fargo, 216 West Ave

Concord
Wells Fargo, 50 Union St N

Raleigh
PNC, 301 Fayetteville St
Wells Fargo, 150 Fayetteville St; & 500 S. Salisbury St (ATM only)
Bank of America, 421 Fayetteville St
BB&T, 434 Fayetteville St
First Citizens, 239 Fayetteville St

Rocky Mount
PNC, 131 N. Church St
Wells Fargo, 100 N. Church St (ATM only)

Salisbury
Wells Fargo, 130 S. Main St

Selma
BB&T, 212 N. Raiford St
First Citizens, 114 N. Raiford St

Smithfield
First Citizens, 409 E. Market St
Wells Fargo, 201 E. Market St

Southern Pines
Wells Fargo, 600 SW Broad St
Bank of America,105 W. Morganton Rd
BB&T, 200 SW Broad St
First Citizens, 390 SW Broad St

Wilson
Wells Fargo, 301 Nash St NE
BB&T, 223 Nash St W
First Citizens, 400 Atlantic Christian College Dr (Barton College)

Winston-Salem
Wells Fargo, 100 N. Main St;
BB&T, 200 W. 2nd St; & 150 N. Marshall St
Bank of America, 1300 E. 5th St

Appendix C

ENTERPRISE CAR RENTAL

LOCATIONS NEAREST TO TRAIN STATIONS

(not necessarily within walking distance; but car is delivered to your location)

BURLINGTON: 2326 N. CHURCH STREET, BURLINGTON, NC 27217, (336) 229-0336
CARY: 1859-A N. HARRISON AVE, CARY, NC 27513, (919) 677-1266
CHARLOTTE: 325 E 9TH ST, CHARLOTTE, NC 28202, (704) 334-8575
DURHAM: 409 S ROXBORO ST, DURHAM, NC 27701, (919) 682-8720
FAYETTEVILLE: 2625 RAEFORD RD, FAYETTEVILLE, NC 28303, (910) 484-2888
GASTONIA: 4101 E FRANKLIN BLVD, GASTONIA, NC 28056, (704) 824-4484
GREENSBORO: 501 W. LEE STREET, GREENSBORO, NC 27406, (336) 275-1299
HAMLET: 702 E BROAD AVE, **ROCKINGHAM**, NC 28379, (910) 419-9344
HIGH POINT: 500 EASTCHESTER DR, HIGH POINT, NC 27262, (336) 821-4156
KANNAPOLIS: 1421 HIGHWAY 29 NORTH, **CONCORD**, NC 28025, (704) 788-9300
RALEIGH: 431 S MCDOWELL ST, RALEIGH, NC 27601, (919) 833-8788
ROCKY MOUNT: 1910 N WESLEYAN BLVD, ROCKY MOUNT, NC 27804, (252) 972-0233
SALISBURY: 1823 S MAIN ST, SALISBURY, NC 28144, (704) 636-2446
SELMA: 831 N BRIGHTLEAF BLVD, **SMITHFIELD**, NC 27577, (919) 938-2562
SOUTHERN PINES: 1730 US-1 SOUTH, SOUTHERN PINES, NC 28387, (910) 692-3400
WILSON: 1313 WARD BLVD, WILSON, NC 27893-4666, (252) 246-0003

AIRPORT LOCATIONS

(pick up at airport)

CHARLOTTE DOUGLAS (CLT)
4202 AIR RAMP ROAD, CHARLOTTE, NC 28214, (704) 359-8884
PIEDMONT TRIAD (GSO)
GREENSBORO, NC 27409, (336) 662-0188
RALEIGH-DURHAM (RDU)
1008 RENTAL CAR DR, RDU AIRPORT, NC 27623, (919) 840-9555

HIGH POINT AMTRAK STATION, author photo

SOUTHERN PINES AMTRAK STATION, author photo

Appendix D

COLLEGES AND UNIVERSITIES

University	Location	Closest Train Station	Connecting Bus (Local Transit)
Appalachian State	Boone	Greensboro or Charlotte	Coach America (AppalCART)
East Carolina	Greenville	Wilson	Greyhound (GREAT)
Elizabeth City State	Elizabeth City	Wilson	Greyhound
Fayetteville State	Fayetteville	Fayetteville	(FAST)
NC A&T State	Greensboro	Greensboro	(GTA)
North Carolina State	Raleigh	Raleigh	(CAT & Wolfline)
UNC-Asheville	Asheville	Greensboro	Greyhound to Asheville, (ATS)
UNC-Chapel Hill	Chapel Hill	Durham	DATA (CHTS)
UNC-Charlotte	Charlotte	Charlotte	(CATS)
UNC-Greensboro	Greensboro	Greensboro	(GTA)
UNC-Pembroke	Pembroke	Fayetteville	Greyhound to Lumberton
UNC-Wilmington	Wilmington	Wilson	Greyhound (WAVE)
UNC School of Arts	Winston-Salem	High Point	NC Amtrak Connector (WSTA)
Western Carolina	Cullowhee	Greensboro	Greyhound to Asheville
Winston-Salem State	Winston-Salem	High Point	NC Amtrak Connector (WSTA)

Private Universities and Colleges (continued on next two pages)

University (U) or College	Location	Closest Train Station	Connecting Bus (Local Transit)
Barber-Scotia	Concord	Kannapolis	(Rider)
Barton	Wilson	Wilson	(WTS)
Belmont Abbey	Belmont Abbey	Gastonia	-

University (U) or College	Location	Closest Train Station	Connecting Bus (Local Transit)
Bennett	Greensboro	Greensboro	(GTA)
Brevard	Brevard	Greensboro	Greyhound to Asheville
Campbell	Buies Creek	Raleigh or Fayetteville	-
Carolina Christian	Winston-Salem	High Point	NC Amtrak Connector (WSTA)
Catawba	Salisbury	Salisbury	(STS)
Chowan	Murfreesboro	Rocky Mount	Greyhound to Ahoskie
Davidson U.	Davidson	Kannapolis	-
Duke U.	Durham	Durham	(DATA)
Elon U.	Elon	Burlington	-
Gardner-Webb U.	Boiling Springs	Charlotte	Greyhound to Kings Mountain
Greensboro	Greensboro	Greensboro	(GTA)
Guilford	Greensboro	Greensboro	(GTA)
High Point U.	High Point	High Point	(Hi tran)
Johnson C. Smith U.	Charlotte	Charlotte	(CATS)
Johnson & Wales U.	Charlotte	Charlotte	(CATS)
Laurel U.	High Point	High Point	(Hi tran)
Lees-McRae	Banner Elk	Greensboro	Coach America to Boone
Lenoir-Rhyne	Hickory	Greensboro	Greyhound to Hickory
Livingstone	Salisbury	Salisbury	(STS)
Louisburg	Louisburg	Raleigh	-
Mars Hill	Mars Hill	Greensboro	Greyhound to Asheville
Meredith	Raleigh	Raleigh	(CAT)
Methodist U.	Fayetteville	Fayetteville	(FAST)
Mid-Atlantic Christian U.	Elizabeth City	Wilson	Greyhound to Elizabeth City
Montreat	Black Mountain	Greensboro	Greyhound to Asheville
Mount Olive	Mount Olive	Wilson	Greyhound to Goldsboro
New Life Theo. Sem.	Charlotte	Charlotte	(CATS)
NC Wesleyan	Rocky Mount	Rocky Mount	-

University (U) or College	Location	Closest Train Station	Connecting Bus (Local Transit)
Pfeiffer	Misenheimer	Salisbury	-
Piedmont Baptist	Winston-Salem	High Point	NC Amtrak Connector (WSTA)
Queen's	Charlotte	Charlotte	(CATS)
Salem	Winston-Salem	High Point	NC Amtrak Connector (WSTA)
St. Andrews Presbyterian	Laurinburg	Fayetteville or Charlotte	Coach America to Laurinburg
St. Augustine's	Raleigh	Raleigh	(CAT)
School of Communication Arts	Raleigh (nr. Wake Forest)	Raleigh	-
Shaw U.	Raleigh	Raleigh	(CAT)
SE Baptist Theo. Sem.	Wake Forest	Raleigh	-
SE Free Will Baptist	Wendell	Raleigh	-
Wake Forest U.	Winston-Salem	High Point	NC Amtrak Connector (WSTA)
Warren Wilson	Swannanoa	Greensboro	Greyhound to Asheville
William Peace U.	Raleigh	Raleigh	(CAT)
Wingate U.	Wingate	Charlotte	Coach America to Monroe

RALEIGH AMTRAK STATION, "CITY OF GREENSBORO" #1810, author photo

WINSTON-SALEM TRANSPORTATION CENTER, author photo

COMFORT, PIEDMONT TRAIN STYLE, author photo

Appendix E

TRANSPORTATION OPERATORS

(**Bolded** communities also have NC Amtrak passenger train service)

• LOCAL PUBLIC TRANSIT

Asheville	ATS	www.ashevillenc.gov/transit
Boone	AppalCART	www.appalcart.com
Cary	C/Tran	www.townofcary.org
Chapel Hill	CHT	www.townofchapelhill.org
Charlotte	CATS	www.ridetransit.org
Durham	DATA	data.durhamnc.gov
Fayetteville	FAST	www.ridefast.net
Gastonia	GTS	www.cityofgastonia.com
Greensboro	GTA	www.greensboro-nc.gov
Greenville	GREAT	www.greenvillenc.gov
Hickory	Greenway	www.mygreenway.org
High Point	Hi tran	www.high-point.net/hi-tran
Kannapolis/Concord	Rider	www.ckrider.com
Raleigh	CAT	www.raleighnc.gov/transit
Rocky Mount	TRT	www.rockymountnc.gov/trt
Salisbury	STS	www.salisburync.gov/transit
Wilmington	WAVE	www.wavetransit.com
Wilson	WTS	www.wilsonnc.org
Winston-Salem (Connector)	WSTS	www.wstransit.com

• REGIONAL PUBLIC TRANSIT

Triangle	Triangle Transit	www.triangletransit.org, www.gotriangle.org
Piedmont Triad	PART	www.partnc.org

• GREYHOUND

www.greyhound.com

Serving: Ahoskie, Asheville, **Charlotte**, Concord (**Kannapolis)**, **Durham**, Edenton, Elizabeth City, **Fayetteville**, **Gastonia**, Goldsboro, **Greensboro**, Greenville, Henderson, Hickory, **High Point**, Jacksonville, Kings Mountain, Kinston, Lumberton, **Raleigh**, **Rocky Mount**, **Salisbury**, Smithfield (**Selma**), Statesville, Wallace, Washington, Williamston, Wilmington, **Wilson**, & Winston-Salem

• COACH AMERICA

www.coachamerica.com

Serving: Blowing Rock, Boone, **Charlotte**, **Fayetteville**, **Gastonia**, Hickory, Laurinburg, Lenoir, Lincolnton, Monroe, Rockingham, & Wadesboro.

• NCDOT

Provides equipment and covers operating costs of Piedmont trains (#73, 74, 75 & 76)
Equipment list: www.bytrain.org/equipmt.html

INTERIOR OF NCDOT'S PIEDMONT COACHES, author photo

CHARLOTTE LYNX LIGHT RAIL TRAIN, author photo

Appendix F

CHARLOTTE'S LIGHT RAIL SYSTEM, LYNX BLUE LINE

An attraction in itself by being North Carolina's first modern urban rail system, the almost 10-mile LYNX Blue Line connects the Center City (Uptown) with I-485 at South Blvd. The 15 stations (see map below) are served 7 days a week from 5:30am through 1:30am. Weekday train frequencies are 10 minutes during the peak hours, and 15 minutes off-peak. On weekends, trains operate every 20 minutes during the day and every 30 minutes during late night hours. For up-to-the minute details, go to: http://charmeck.org/city/charlotte/cats/lynx/Pages/default.aspx

Charlotte Area Transit System, CATS
LYNX Blue Route Light Rail

- 7th St
- Charlotte Transportation Center
- 3rd St, Convention Center
- Stonewall
- Carson
- Bland
- East / West Blvd
- New Bern
- [P] Scaleybark
- [P] Woodlawn
- [P] Tyvola
- [P] Archdale
- [P] Arrowood
- [P] Sharon Rd West
- [P] I-485, South Blvd

[P] Park and Ride Station

CHARLOTTE LYNX LIGHT RAIL TRAIN AT STATION, author photo

CHARLOTTE TRANSPORTATION CENTER, author photo

Appendix G

CHECKING TRAIN STATUS ON YOUR LAPTOP, TABLET OR SMART PHONE

On Amtrak's website, there is an application for you to check the status of your train, i.e., is it on time; if late, how much late, etc.). The appearance of the website on your mobile device will be different from what you would see on a desktop PC, but the data entry is the same.

Step 1: Go to www.amtrak.com

Step 2: Click on the tab "STATUS" found to the left of the page

Step 3: Enter the Train Number from your ticket, and either the "From" station name or three-letter code or the "To" station name of three-letter code; or both the "From" and "To" stations, and then click on the "CHECK STATUS" button. You should then be taken to a page that gives you the information you require. Three-letter station codes (similar but not the same as airport codes) for North Carolina stations are listed below.

EXAMPLE
Let's say you are traveling from Greensboro to Charlotte. To find out your train's arrival time in Greensboro without the Train Number, simply enter "GRO" for the "From" station and "CLT" for the "To" station, and select "Scheduled Depart." Based on your not having entered a train number, your will be given information for several trains that have either not yet reached Greensboro or are not scheduled to depart their origin station until later in the day. Scroll down until you see your train's information, which will include the scheduled and anticipated arrival times.

AMTRAK CODES FOR NORTH CAROLINA STATIONS

Burlington	BNC	High Point	HPT
Cary	CYN	Kannapolis	KAN
Charlotte	CLT	Raleigh	RGH
Durham	DNC	Rocky Mount	RMT
Fayetteville	FAY	Salisbury	SAL
Gastonia	GAS	Selma	SSM
Greensboro	GRO	Southern Pines	SOP
Hamlet	HAM	Wilson	WLN

"CITY OF BURLINGTON" #1893 LOCOMOTIVE CHRISTENING, 2011, author photo

GREENSBORO AMTRAK STATION INTERIOR, author photo

Index

Ahoskie, 25 (map), 65, 77
Antiques, 51
AppalCART (Boone), 25 (map), 77
Art Galleries, 52
Asheville, 25 (map), 65, 77
ATS (Asheville), 75
Banks (App. B), 69
Blowing Rock, 25 (map), 65, 77
Boone, 25 (map), 65, 77
Breweries, 53
Burlington, 27
Car Rental (App. C), 71
Cary, 28
C/Tran (Cary), 77
CAT (Raleigh), 77
CATS (Charlotte), 77
Cemeteries, 58
Chapel Hill, 64, 77
Charlotte, 31
Charlotte Douglas Int'l Airport, 8
CHT (Chapel Hill), 77
Churches, 54
Coach America, 77
Colleges (App. D), 73
Concord, 39
DATA, 75
Durham, 32
Edenton, 25 (map), 65, 77
Elizabeth City, 25 (map), 65, 77
Emergency Medical Treatment
FAST (Fayetteville), 77
Fayetteville, 33
Festivals & Shows, 56
Gardens, 57
Gastonia, 35
Goldsboro, 25 (map), 65, 77
GREAT, 77
Greensboro, 36
Greenville, 25 (map), 65, 77
Greenway (Hickory), 77
Greyhound Lines, 77
GTA (Greensboro), 77
GTS (Gastonia), 77
Hamlet, 37
Henderson , 25 (map), 65, 77
Hickory, 25 (map), 65, 77
High Point, 38
Hi tran (High Point), 77
Jacksonville, 25 (map), 65, 77
Kannapolis, 39
Kings Mountain, 25 (map), 65, 77
Kinston, 25 (map), 65, 77
Laurinburg, 25 (map), 65, 77
Lenoir, 25 (map), 65, 77
Lincolnton, 25 (map), 65, 77
LYNX Light Rail (App. F), 79
Monroe, 25 (map), 65, 77
Monuments, 58
New Bern, 25 (map), 65, 77
NCDOT, 77
Parks, 59
PART (Piedmont Triad), 77
Piedmont Triad Int'l Airport, 8
Public Transit Systems (App. E), 77
Raleigh, 40
RDU Int'l Airport, 7
Rider, 75
Rockingham, 25 (map), 65, 77
Rocky Mount, 42
Salisbury, 44
Selma, 45
Smithfield, 25 (map), 65, 77
Sports, 60
Statesville, 25 (map), 65, 77
Statues, 58
STS (Salisbury), 77
Theaters, 61
Train Status (App. G), 81
Triangle Transit, 77
TRT (Rocky Mount), 77

Universities, (App. D), 73
Urgent Care Clinics, 62
Visitors Bureaus (App. A), 67
Wadesboro, 25 (map), 65, 77
Wallace, 25 (map), 65, 77
Washington, 25 (map), 65, 77
Williamston, 25 (map), 65, 77
WAVE (Wilmington), 77
Wilmington, 25 (map), 65, 77
Wilson, 47
Winston-Salem, 49
WSTS (Winston-Salem), 77

www.ingramcontent.com/pod-product-compliance
Ingram Content Group UK Ltd.
Pitfield, Milton Keynes, MK11 3LW, UK
UKHW041923190726
13854UKWH00003B/1407